# CAMBRIDGE LIBRARY COLLECTION

*Books of enduring scholarly value*

## Travel and Exploration

The history of travel writing dates back to the Bible, Caesar, the Vikings and the Crusaders, and its many themes include war, trade, science and recreation. Explorers from Columbus to Cook charted lands not previously visited by Western travellers, and were followed by merchants, missionaries, and colonists, who wrote accounts of their experiences. The development of steam power in the nineteenth century provided opportunities for increasing numbers of 'ordinary' people to travel further, more economically, and more safely, and resulted in great enthusiasm for travel writing among the reading public. Works included in this series range from first-hand descriptions of previously unrecorded places, to literary accounts of the strange habits of foreigners, to examples of the burgeoning numbers of guidebooks produced to satisfy the needs of a new kind of traveller - the tourist.

## The Life and Acts of
## Don Alonzo Enriquez de Guzman

The publications of the Hakluyt Society (founded in 1846) made available edited (and sometimes translated) early accounts of exploration. The first series, which ran from 1847 to 1899, consists of 100 books containing published or previously unpublished works by authors from Christopher Columbus to Sir Francis Drake, and covering voyages to the New World, to China and Japan, to Russia and to Africa and India. This sixteenth-century autobiographical narrative, translated and published in 1862 from a manuscript in the National Library of Madrid and interspersed with contemporary letters, gives the self-justificatory account of the adventures and misadventures of an impecunious Spanish nobleman whose efforts to make a fortune took him all round Europe and eventually to Peru, where he was witness to the feud between Pizarro and Almagro which had lasting consequences for the future of South America. An introductory essay places this account in the context of other histories of the Spanish conquest.

T0382119

Cambridge University Press has long been a pioneer in the reissuing of out-of-print titles from its own backlist, producing digital reprints of books that are still sought after by scholars and students but could not be reprinted economically using traditional technology. The Cambridge Library Collection extends this activity to a wider range of books which are still of importance to researchers and professionals, either for the source material they contain, or as landmarks in the history of their academic discipline.

Drawing from the world-renowned collections in the Cambridge University Library, and guided by the advice of experts in each subject area, Cambridge University Press is using state-of-the-art scanning machines in its own Printing House to capture the content of each book selected for inclusion. The files are processed to give a consistently clear, crisp image, and the books finished to the high quality standard for which the Press is recognised around the world. The latest print-on-demand technology ensures that the books will remain available indefinitely, and that orders for single or multiple copies can quickly be supplied.

The Cambridge Library Collection will bring back to life books of enduring scholarly value (including out-of-copyright works originally issued by other publishers) across a wide range of disciplines in the humanities and social sciences and in science and technology.

# The Life and Acts of Don Alonzo Enriquez de Guzman

*A Knight of Seville, of the Order of Santiago,
A.D. 1518 to 1543*

Clements R. Markham

CAMBRIDGE
UNIVERSITY PRESS

CAMBRIDGE UNIVERSITY PRESS

Cambridge, New York, Melbourne, Madrid, Cape Town, Singapore,
São Paolo, Delhi, Dubai, Tokyo, Mexico City

Published in the United States of America by Cambridge University Press, New York

www.cambridge.org
Information on this title: www.cambridge.org/9781108010702

This edition first published 1862
This digitally printed version 2010

ISBN 978-1-108-01070-2 Paperback

WORKS ISSUED BY

# The Hakluyt Society.

---

THE LIFE AND ACTS OF DON ALONZO

ENRIQUEZ DE GUZMAN.

M.DCCCLXII.

# LIFE AND ACTS

OF

# DON ALONZO ENRIQUEZ DE GUZMAN,

A KNIGHT OF SEVILLE, OF THE ORDER OF SANTIAGO,

A.D. 1518 TO 1543.

TRANSLATED

FROM AN ORIGINAL AND INEDITED MANUSCRIPT
IN THE NATIONAL LIBRARY AT MADRID;

WITH NOTES AND AN INTRODUCTION,

BY

CLEMENTS R. MARKHAM, F.S.A., F.R.G.S.,

CORR. MEM. OF THE UNIVERSITY OF CHILE.
AUTHOR OF " CUZCO AND LIMA."

LONDON:

PRINTED FOR THE HAKLUYT SOCIETY

M.DCCC.LXII.

# THE HAKLUYT SOCIETY.

# TABLE OF CONTENTS.

*b*

# INTRODUCTION.

THE document from which the following translation has been made is amongst the original and inedited manuscripts in the National Library at Madrid (*Papeles MSS. originales y ineditos*, *G.* 127). The manuscript consists of a life of Don Alonzo Enriquez de Guzman, a native of Seville, of good family, written by himself, and interspersed with numerous letters, comprising a period between 1518 and 1543, from his nineteenth to his forty-fourth year. His very curious and interesting narrative includes his adventures in Spain, Sicily, Italy, Germany, Flanders, the Balearic Isles, and Peru; and it is one of the very few works in which the feuds of the Pizarros and Almagro are described by an eye-witness. Moreover, with the exception of Pedro Pizarro, and possibly Cieza de Leon, Don Alonzo is the earliest traveller in Peru whose writings have come down to us. For this reason the manuscript appeared to me to be worth translating, and thus taking its place in the series of the Hakluyt Society's works; more especially as it had escaped the notice of Mr. Prescott, and others who have written on the discovery and conquest of Peru.

I am indebted for a knowledge of this curious
manuscript to my friend Don Benjamin Vicuña
Mackenna, an eminent Chilian writer and politician,
whose works have in no small degree increased the
literary reputation of the vigorous and robust little
republic, which nestles at the feet of the mighty
cordillera of the southern Andes.[1]  He came upon it

[1] Don Benjamin Vicuña Mackenna, born in Chile in August
1831, is the grandson of Don F. Ramon Vicuña, who was President of the Republic of Chile in 1829, and died in 1849.  The
Vicuñas are of an ancient Biscayan family.  Don Benjamin's
mother was a daughter of the Irish General Mackenna, of county
Monaghan, who fought for Chilian independence.  In 1851 Don
Benjamin was imprisoned and banished for his share in the rebellion of General Cruz.  He sailed to California, and travelled thence
through Mexico, the United States, England, and continental
Europe; studying for a year in an agricultural college at Ciren-
cester.  In 1854 he returned, by Buenos Ayres and the Pampas,
to Chile, and commenced an active literary career in Santiago.
He became Secretary to a Chilian Agricultural Society, and editor
of their journal.  He also published a history of that portion of
the Chilian struggle for independence which is comprised in the
romantic adventures of the brothers Carrera (*El Ostracismo de los
Carreras.*  Santiago.  1857), a narrative of his travels, and a life
of his grandfather, General Mackenna.  In 1858 he became an
active opponent of the Chilian President Montt's Administration,
and edited a newspaper which advocated the convocation of a
Constituent Assembly to reform the Constitution.  At last, in
January 1859, Vicuña, with his friends, Custodio Gallo (a rich
Copiapo miner) and the brothers Matta, one a poet of some emi-
nence, and the other a Deputy of Congress, convoked a meeting
of liberals in the Philharmonic Hall of Santiago.  The Government
forbade the meeting, and the four friends were thrown into prison.
After three months, they were hurried down to Valparaiso and put
on board the English barque *Louisa Braginton*, the captain of

accidentally, while employed in collecting materials in Spain for a life of Don Diego de Almagro, the discoverer of his native land. The manuscript is merely entered in the list as—" *Libro de la vida de Don Alonzo Enriquez de Guzman ;*" so that it is not surprising that others, in searching for materials for a history of the discovery and conquest of Peru, should not have previously become acquainted with it. I took the opportunity, during a visit to Madrid in the autumn of 1861, on business connected with the public service, of examining this manuscript in the national library ; and I came to the conclusion that it was worthy of being brought from the obscurity in which it has been buried for more than three cen-

which had received two thousand dollars to put them on shore at Liverpool. They suffered very much during the voyage from wretched accommodation and bad provisions, and, on their arrival in England, they brought an action against the captain for false imprisonment. During his second visit to Europe, Vicuña went to Spain, and was engaged in collecting materials for a life of Al-magro the discoverer of Chile, in the libraries of Madrid. In December 1859 he returned to South America and took up his abode at Lima, where he completed a life of General O'Higgins, the hero of Chilian independence (*El Ostracismo de General Don Bernardo O'Higgins, escrito sobre Documentos ineditos y noticias autenticas.* Valparaiso, 1860), and a history of the first two years of the war of independence in Peru. On the election of Perez, the present President of Chile, in 1861, Vicuña was enabled to return to Chile, and he is, I understand, instituting proceedings against Don Manuel Montt, the late President, for his summary and ille-gal transportation. It is to be hoped that he will now have leisure to arrange his rich materials, and complete his life of Almagro,— a most important addition to the literature of Spanish conquest in America.

turies. Whatever may be thought of the author of
this strange autobiography, it certainly contains a
great deal which is very curious and amusing, while
the latter half forms a very important addition to our
knowledge of the famous feud between Pizarro and
Almagro, which followed so closely on their conquest
of the rich land of the Incas.

Our author, Don Alonzo Enriquez de Guzman,
was a native of Seville, of good family, and was born
some time in the year 1500. On his father's side he
was descended from an illegitimate son of Henry II,
King of Castile; and his great grandfather, after
doing good service in the Moorish wars, eventually
settled in Seville, and obtained the hand of a sister of
the first Duke of Medina Sidonia.

Young Don Alonzo's veins were very well supplied
with the *sangre azul*, but his purse was not equally
well supplied with money; so, having first taken to
himself a young wife named Constance de Añasco,
he set out from Seville to seek his fortune when only
eighteen years of age. I find him mentioned in the
work of Lopez de Haro, in the following short sentence—"Don Alonzo Enriquez, eldest son of Don
Garcia, by his second wife Dona Catalina de Guevara,
was married in Seville to Dona Constança Añasco, by
whom he had no children."[1]

Like most penniless young men of good family in

---

[1] *Nobiliario Genealogico de los Reyes y Titulos de España, com-
puesto por Alonzo Lopez de Haro.* Madrid, 1622, i, p. 28. For
an account of Don Alonzo's family see note at page 5, and note at
page 55.

those days, he made for the Court, which was then at Barcelona, in the hope of obtaining some post with large pay and little work; and, like most others, he was doomed to disappointment. He then enlisted as a soldier in an expedition which was sent against a Moorish island on the coast of Africa, between Tunis and Tripoli; and his subsequent adventures in Sicily, Naples, Rome, Cologne, and Valenciennes; his desperate exploit on board a ship off Alicante; his services in the Balearic islands; and his life at the Spanish court of Charles V, occupy about half the manuscript. His own violent conduct had made him many enemies, and involved him in difficulties; and at last, in 1534, he resolved to seek his fortune in the Indies. He arrived in Peru at a critical period of the conquest, and he was a principal actor in the events which took place between the departure of the Adelantado Almagro for Chile in the summer of 1535, and his execution in July 1538.

I have omitted a portion of the manuscript, which precedes the account of Don Alonzo's voyage to the Indies, as it is entirely occupied with his litigations and quarrels in Seville. These are very tedious, and could not possibly have any interest for a reader of the present day.

Don Alonzo's accounts of the transactions which took place during these three years, which are included in his narrative, his letter to Charles V, and his denunciation of Hernando Pizarro, are exceedingly important; for, with the possible exception of

c

Pedro Pizarro, he is the only eye-witness of the events he describes, whose testimony has been preserved to us. I find him mentioned by Garcilasso Inca de la Vega as one of the bravest knights amongst the defenders of Cuzco against the Indian army of Inca Manco;[1] and he himself tells us that he was " maestro de campo " during the siege, and supplies several interesting particulars respecting the subsequent seizure of Cuzco by Almagro, on his return from Chile. Indeed, he is accused of having betrayed Hernando Pizarro, and delivered up the city to his rival.[2] When Alonzo de Alvarado advanced from Lima, our author was sent, with others, to open a negotiation, and he was an eye-witness of the battle of Abancay. He was afterwards nominated by Almagro as one of the commissioners to treat with Pizarro respecting the boundary of their respective governments; and both Garcilasso de la Vega and Pizarro y Orellana, in his " Varones illustres del nuevo mundo," mention him as having acted in that capacity.[3] Thus he was present at all the transactions which followed at Mala and Chincha, accompanied Almagro in his retreat to the interior, was in Cuzco when the battle of Las Salinas was fought, and witnessed the death of his old friend Almagro, who nominated him as one of his executors. Pizarro

---

[1] *Commentarios Reales.* Pte. ii, lib. ii, cap. xxiv.

[2] *Varones Illustres,* p. 223.

[3] *Commentarios Reales.* Pte. ii, lib. ii, cap. xxxv. *Varones Illustres del Nuevo Mundo, por Don Fernando Pizarro y Orellana, Cavallero de la orden de Calatrava.* Madrid, 1639, p. 178.

y Orellana states that he betrayed a design to rescue Almagro, to his enemy Hernando Pizarro,[1] but this is grossly improbable, and we know that the author of the "Varones illustres" was a strong partizan of the Pizarros, and likely to take every opportunity of blackening the friends of their unfortunate rival.

I have not succeeded in finding the name of Don Alonzo Enriquez de Guzman mentioned in any other Spanish work.

To appreciate the value of Don Alonzo's narrative of events in Peru it will be necessary to recapitulate the authorities which are accessible to the general reader, and on which the history of Spanish discovery and conquest in Peru are founded. The three earliest are the works of Augustin de Zarate, Francisco Lopez de Gomara, and Pedro Cieza de Leon. Zarate went out as accountant with the Viceroy Blasco Nuñez de Vela in 1543; and his "History of the Conquest" appeared at Antwerp in 1555. Gomara, the author of the "Historia de las Indias," was never in the New World; and Cieza de Leon, who wrote the "Cronica del Peru," went to Peru when only fifteen, served with Gasca in his campaign against Gonzalo Pizarro, and completed his work, which is more an itinerary than a history, in 1550. But the two most valuable authorities on the civil wars which immediately succeeded the Peruvian conquest are Pedro Pizarro and the Inca Garcilasso de la Vega. The former went out as a page to his relative Francisco the Conqueror in 1529, remained with him until

---

[1] *Varones Illustres,* p. 325.

his assassination, afterwards settled at Arequipa, and completed his work, " Relaciones del Descubrimento y Conquista de los Reynos del Peru," in 1571. It is the narrative of a rough half-educated soldier, and occupies much the same place in the history of the conquest of Peru as the work of Bernal Diaz does in that of Mexico. Bernal Diaz was, however, a much finer fellow than Pedro Pizarro.

Garcilasso de la Vega had better means of information than any of the other writers of the period respecting the events comprised in Don Alonzo's narrative. He was born at Cuzco; and though his birth did not take place until 1540, two years after the death of Almagro, yet he derived his information from the most original sources. His mother was an Inca princess ; and his father, coming to Peru with the Adelantado Pedro de Alvarado, was an eye-witness of most of the transactions from that time until the rout of Gonzalo Pizarro at Sacsahuana, when he deserted to the army of Gasca. The younger Garcilasso went to Spain in 1560, and published the two parts of his work in 1609 and 1616, the year of his death. He quotes largely from Zarate and Gomara, while he supplies an immense store of information from the traditions of his mother's family and the recollections of his father's conversations, and his work is by far the most interesting of all those which treat of the conquest of Peru, and the former civilization of the Incas.

In the century after that of the conquest, two histories of very unequal value were published, those of Montesinos and Herrera. The " Anales" of the

Licentiate Fernando Montesinos, who was twice sent to Peru officially, are, owing to the untrustworthiness of the writer, of very slight value; while the "Historia General de las Indias" of Antonio de Herrera, the first four decades of which were published in 1601, and the second four in 1615, should rank only second to the "Commentarios Reales" of Garcilasso de la Vega. Herrera wrote in an agreeable style, and he was indefatigable in collecting authentic materials for his work. Some years afterwards the "Varones Illustres del Nuevo Mundo" were published by Pizarro y Orellana, a relation of the Conqueror's family; and this work contains some additional information, although its authority is marred by the violent bias of the author in favour of the Pizarro faction.

The "Historia del Peru" of Diego Fernandez de Palencia, which was published at Seville in 1571, only gives an account of the campaign of Gasca against Gonzalo Pizarro, and of the rebellion of Giron; and the author did not go to Peru until long after the death of Almagro.[1]

[1] Mr. Prescott also mentions three manuscripts, by Oviedo, Sarmiento, and Ondegardo, to which I have not had access; but they do not include any account of the period during which our author was in Peru.

Don Juan Sarmiento, who was President of the Council of the Indies from 1563 to 1565, was at Cuzco in 1550, and wrote a history of the Incas, which, however, ends at the conquest.

The licentiate Polo de Ondegardo was in Peru during the war between Gonzalo Pizarro and the Viceroy Blasco Nuñez, was for some years Corregidor of Cuzco, and prepared his "Relaciones,"

Thus, of all the above authorities, Zarate, Gomara, Cieza de Leon, Pedro Pizarro, Garcilasso de la Vega, Montesinos, Herrera, Pizarro y Orellana, and Fernandez, only one was in Peru at the same time as our author, Don Alonzo, and none acted so important a part in the scenes which they describe.

Don Alonzo Enriquez de Guzman, as an eye witness, may therefore be considered as the most original authority for all events in Peruvian history from the commencement of the siege of Cuzco, in 1534, to the execution of Almagro in 1538. I have carefully compared his version of the transactions in Peru at that period with the accounts given by Garcilasso de la Vega, (and his authorities, Zarate and Gomara), Herrera, and Pizarro y Orellana ; and I find that, in all the main points, they agree to a remarkable extent.

Immediately after the death of Almagro our author returned to Spain, and he continues his journal for two years longer, when the manuscript abruptly terminates in the middle of a letter. I have failed in my endeavours to find any further traces of Don Alonzo, and I am therefore ignorant of the time or place of his death ; but it is almost certain that his great enemy, Hernando Pizarro, who attained the extraordinary age of a hundred years, survived to see

being an account of the laws and customs of the Incas, between 1561 and 1571.

Gonzalo Fernandez de Oviedo wrote a history which only goes down to the return of Almagro from Chile.

our author pass away, with the rest of the generation which witnessed the conquest of Peru, and the feuds of the conquerors.

Of the value of the geographical information supplied by Don Alonzo very little can be said; but at the same time the remarks of a traveller, however meagre they may be, who visited several of the countries of the new world so very soon after their discovery, must necessarily possess an interest which cannot be claimed for the more elaborate narratives of a later date.

It is not possible to make out the dates at which the different parts of the narrative were written, though, from an expression in the dedication, it seems likely that the first half was composed before Don Alonzo sailed for the Indies; and he expressly states that the dedication itself was written during the voyage. The Peruvian part was evidently jotted down from time to time as opportunity offered; and the latter portion of the manuscript is in a very incomplete and unfinished state. Of course it cannot have been intended for publication in its present form, and either death or some other cause must have stepped in to prevent Don Alonzo from correcting and completing it. Yet it is fortunate that we have received it, before it was polished, and smoothed over by the last finishing touches from the hand of the author; for now we see Don Alonzo as he really was; his faults, and even his crimes, told so naïvely by himself, make him far more companionable than if he had written more on his guard; and the occa-

sional contradictions, the motives for which are so
transparent, enable us to ascertain the truth with
comparative ease.

Don Alonzo was in the unfortunate position of a
very poor man of a very proud and noble family.
The life of a penniless adventurer, seeking his fortune, is not calculated to bring out the best qualities
of our nature. In his youth he was a debauched
unscrupulous young ruffian, in the prime of life a
querulous discontented hanger-on of the court, and
the most creditable part of his life was passed amidst
the dangers and hardships of the civil war in Peru.
He confesses to much meanness, and occasional vil-
lanies; yet there was some good in this half-tamed
child of Andalusia. He performed many acts of
kindness; he had many warm and constant friends,
a sure sign that he was not altogether a bad man;
and his bravery and gallant conduct before the
enemy, of which he tells us sufficient himself, is confirmed by the independent and impartial testimony
of Garcilasso Inca de la Vega. Much excuse must
be made for a half-educated orphan, much in consideration of the age in which he lived.

On the whole, Don Alonzo Enriquez de Guzman
may be taken as an average specimen of a young
Spanish adventurer of family during the sixteenth
century. He was certainly as brave, more honourable, and less cruel than most of the Spanish knights
who flocked to the ill-fated land of the Incas, after
its conquest by Pizarro; and, as such, I now beg
to introduce him to the subscribers to the Hakluyt
Society.

I may add that I have myself personally visited and carefully inspected most of the places memorable as the scenes of events which took place after the conquest of Peru, during the civil wars of the Pizarros and Almagros, many of which are mentioned by Don Alonzo. I was several months at Cuzco. I have visited the coast valleys of Mala, Chincha, Pisco, Yca and Nasca, have ascended the pass of Huaytara, and have carefully examined the battle fields of Abancay, Las Salinas, Chupas, Sacsahuana, Chuquinga, and Pucara.

# BOOK

OF

## *THE LIFE AND ACTS*

OF

# DON ALONZO ENRIQUEZ DE GUZMAN,

### OF SEVILLE,

A NOBLE KNIGHT OF THE ORDER OF SANTIAGO.

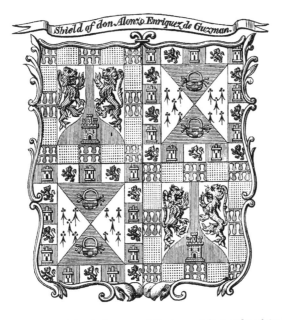

*Quarterly, first and fourth the arms of Enriquez of Portugal and Seville ; second and third the arms of Guzman, in a bordure of the royal lions and castles.*

# TO THE READER.

---

*THE present work was composed by a knight, in imitation of that of Cæsar. This knight left his country to acquire glory and renown in foreign lands, that his name might be had in perpetual memory. In this work will be found many things very healthful for the soul, and for the honour and safety of the body. You will find in it matter of great moment and notoriety. You will read letters from our Emperor himself, who now reigns, to the author, and also the author's dispatches to his sacred and Catholic Majesty, and to other persons, for the author held the office of gentleman in the royal palace. It is a very instructive and edifying work for all sorts and conditions of persons, treating of a great variety of subjects, both entertaining and important, and the author not only relates what happened to himself, but also what he saw and heard. Know then, O most inquisitive reader that, if you are curious to learn the transactions of the governments of this world, I am able to say, with truth, as regards this my writing, that I saw what I wrote, and I wrote what I saw.*

*Farewell.*

# DEDICATION.

MOST ILLUSTRIOUS SIRE.

When our God manifested his greatness in the
creation of all things, he so ordered and arranged them that,
for the preservation of the rest, the superiors should have
the rule and governance over the inferiors, as the natural
philosophers and sacred theologians prove, without which
the order of things could not be preserved. Thus, most
illustrious Sire, I find that if the works produced by the
labour and anxiety of those who have written, and shall
write, do not find favour with the great, they very soon
perish. Mindful of this, I do not know in Spain, most

[1] This Don Juan Alonzo Perez de Guzman succeeded his brother, as
sixth Duke of Medina Sidonia, and eighth Count of Niebla. His son,
Don Juan Claros de Guzman, who is alluded to in the dedication, died
in his father's lifetime, and on the death of the sixth duke, his grandson, Alonzo Perez de Guzman, who was Captain-General of Milan, Commander of the Armada sent against England, and employed on other
important services, during the reign of Philip II, succeeded as seventh
duke. He died in A.D. 1615.

The author, Don Alonzo Enriquez de Guzman, was descended from a
daughter of the second Count of Niebla, and was, therefore, a third
cousin of the Duke of Medina Sidonia, to whom he dedicated his work.

illustrious Sire, one to whom I ought with more propriety to dedicate this work than to your Worship ; and this for many reasons. First, on account of what I know of your kindness, and your inclination to virtue ; second, because Don Garcia Enriquez de Guzman, my father, was the servant and relation of thine, so that we are also relations, and as such you may claim my services. You should, most illustrious Sire, take notice of my affairs, and examine them with your sagacious judgment ; as I have done those of your relations, especially of Don Juan Claros, your eldest surviving son. Thirdly, because you are sprung from the most Christian and most faithful knight, Don Alonzo Perez, the good ; who, when he was besieged by Moors, the enemies of our holy Catholic faith, in the castle of Tarifa, and when they had captured his son, and, that they might oblige him to surrender the castle, put him on the ground to behead him, thinking that he would give way to grief for the love of his son, which is the most natural feeling in the world ; loved most the service of God, and loyalty to his king, and, with a great heart, put his hand on his dagger, and with valiant and weighty speech he and his wife said that they had the anvil and hammer wherewith to make another son.[1] The

[1] This Don Alonzo Perez de Guzman, the good, was traditionally the most illustrious ancestor of the great house of Medina Sidonia. He was the third Lord of San Lucar de Barrameda, and grandfather of the first Count of Niebla. Don Alonzo Perez was one of the most famous captains of his age. The circumstance here alluded to by his descendant, is thus related by Alonzo Perez de Haro. " Don Alonzo Perez de Guzman was alcaide of the fortress of Tarifa, when he performed that celebrated act which proved his loyalty to his king, and to the pure blood of his ancestors. Tarifa was besieged by the Infante Don Juan and a large army of Moors, who brought with them Don Pedro de Guzman, the eldest son of Don Alonzo Perez, by his wife, Dona Maria Coronel. The Moors declared they would kill his son if he did not surrender the fortress, and they bound him to a block on the sandy beach in front of Tarifa, ready for execution. Don Alonzo Perez beheld all this from the walls, and his bosom was torn by his paternal love for a dear son so near death ; but he replied to the Infante, that if he had five more sons in

fourth, because your lordship, being the representative according to law, of the most illustrious house of Medina Sidonia, which possesses seventy thousand golden ducats of rent, with many castles and vassals, enjoys all this inheritance like a most Catholic servant of God, and a most faithful vassal of the king. Thus you arrange all your affairs as you think fit. For these reasons it is proper that this little work should be dedicated to you, proceeding, as it does, from the marrow of my understanding. The said work, most illustrious Sire, I therefore beseech that you will accept, for I wrote it not for pomp and vain glory. When this work sees the light, I, by the will of Almighty God, shall have departed this life, and entered into eternal glory.

I date this on the wide ocean, without expecting to see you again, for I go with no thought of returning, in the year of our Lord 1534, and I remain your relation and faithful servant,

Don Alonzo Enriquez de Guzman.

. . . . . . . . .

I dedicated this book after the greater part of it was written, but I did not wish to complete it until I had decided whom I should favour above others.

the same plight, he would deliver them over to death, and even supply the knife, before he would betray his trust. Astonished at such extraordinary heroism, the Infante raised the siege ; and the King Don Sancho granted the tunny fishery to Don Alonzo Perez, as a reward for this great service." In the grant of this fishery he is compared to Abraham, who with equal cheerfulness offered up his son Isaac. Don Alonzo Perez de Guzman was killed in the battle of Gausin, in A.D. 1309, against the Moors, and was buried in the church of San Isidro, in Seville.

Berni relates that Don Alonzo Perez was at dinner when he received the message threatening his son's death, to which he gave a defiant answer. When the news came that his son was actually beheaded, he merely remarked, " My son's death signifies but little, as long as the place is well defended," and went on eating. *Nobiliario Genealogico de Haro*, i, p. 57. *Berni, Creacion de los titulos de Castilla*, p. 121.

# LIFE AND ACTS

# DON ALONZO ENRIQUEZ DE GUZMAN.

## I.

### I BEGIN LIFE.

In the year 1518, being eighteen years of age and nearly nineteen, I found myself fatherless and poor of estate, though rich in lineage, with a mother, who was a very talkative yet honest, good, and pious woman. She was not able to provide for me, seeing that I was growing up, though not of an age to marry, and so from necessity I married.[1] Oppressed with poverty, and desirous of riches, I determined to go in search of adventures, and set out from the city of Seville, which was my native place, with a horse, a mule, a bed, and sixty ducats. I resolved to write down all that happened to me, and not to record anything which is not worthy of credit. My name is Don Alonzo Enriquez de Guzman. I am a descendant of the Count of Gijon, who was son of the King Don Enrique, of Castile. My mother was named Dona Catalina de Guevara.[2]

---

[1] He married a young lady of Seville, named Costança de Añasco, by whom he had no children.

[2] Our author, Don Alonzo Enriquez de Guzman, was the eldest son, by the second marriage, of Don Garcia Enriquez de Guzman, of Seville. By his first wife Don Garcia had two sons, Don Juan de Noroña, and

## II.

I went to Cordova, and to Granada, and to Baeza, where
I met with a captain named Montalvo. He was going to
Italy, and I to the court of the King of Castille, who was in
Barcelona. Our roads were the same as far as Murcia, and
there we had to separate on our respective journeys. At a
distance of four or five leagues from the said city of Baeza,
where we met, we went to pass the night at an inn. Here I
forgot my sixty ducats, which I had placed at my bed-head,
so that the said captain was able to take them while I went
outside, for some purpose which I now forget, for he had
come in to awake me. What with his haste and my care-
lessness, we set out without my missing the purse, and
having gone two leagues I remembered it, but not where I
had left it. I, therefore, went back to look for it with great

Don Garcia de Noroña, who married and settled in the island of Madeira, and the former was the founder of a family there. By his second
wife, Catalina de Guevara, Don Garcia had four sons : first, Don Alonzo,
our author ; second, Don Luis, who was some time in the Brazils, went
as captain of a galleon to India, married a Portuguese lady named
Leonora Correa, and had several children ; third, Don Juan ; and
fourth, Don Fernando. There were also three illegitimate sons.

Don Garcia Enriquez de Guzman, our author's father, was son of
Don Juan Enriquez, and grandson of Don Diego Enriquez, who married
Beatriz de Guzman, daughter of the second Count of Niebla, and sister
of the first Duke of Medina Sidonia. (The duke was born in 1414, and
created duke by King John II in 1445). This Don Diego Enriquez,
who was a knight of Santiago, after serving many years against the
Moors of Granada, finally settled in Seville. He was a natural son of
Don Alonzo Enriquez de Castilla, who was created Count of Noroña and
Gijon in 1373, and, having been in rebellion against his half brother,
King John I, and his nephew, King Henry III, eventually fled into
France. This Count of Gijon was a natural son of Henry II, King of
Castile, by Dona Elvira Iniguez de la Vega.

Our author could also trace his descent from the kings of Castile,
through the Guzmans : the mother of his ancestor, the second Count of
Niebla, having been Beatriz de Castilla, daughter of King Henry II.

haste and no less anxiety. When I reached the inn I sought advice from the captain, who said to me : " Console yourself, that the first mishap that has befallen you is not greater than the loss of sixty dollars, and that you have still got your horse, which you can sell, and I, for the sake of your company, will give you something to eat while you sell it at your ease." After thanking him for his kindness and courtesy, I replied: " I am not able to sell it at my ease, for I intend to appear before the King, with whom I go to live." He then said that he could supply a remedy for my misfortune, for that, near at hand, there was a great lord named the Marques de los Velez, Don Pedro Fajardo,[1] in a place which we had to pass next day, called Velez el Blanco. " If," he continued, " you are the person you represent yourself to be, relate your misfortune, and I have no doubt but that it will be remedied." Next day we arrived at the place, and I went before the Marquis, and related my misfortune in the best way I could, and with as much sorrow as I was able to depict. I then besought him, for mercy's sake, to help me, and he said he would ; but two days passed without his doing so, though not for want of asking. Seeing that he would not help me, I gave him a petition in writing, the tenor of which was as follows : " Most illustrious and best of lords, the other day I spoke to your lordship on the subject of giving me assistance to continue my journey, relating my misfortunes and stating who I am. For the love of God, if you have any doubt, ask Ortiz, your carver, who

---

[1] The first Marques de los Velez was Don Pedro Fajardo, created by Juana the Mad in 1505. He was hereditary adelantado mayor of Murcia, an office granted to his mother's family by John II. His maternal grandfather, Pedro Fajardo, adelantado of Murcia, married Leonora, daughter of Don Rodrigo Manrique, Count of Paredes. The first Marques de los Velez served in the Alpujarras against the Moors, in the time of Ferdinand and Isabella, and afterwards in the wars of Charles V. His son, Don Luis, the second Marquis, was captain-general of Valencia under Philip II. *Berni*, p. 202 ; *Haro*, ii, p. 342.

was my father's page. I shall be satisfied with ten ducats, which I will return to you." He answered that he would see what he could do hereafter, but that at present he could do nothing. The said carver, however, gave me two ducats out of his poor purse. I then went to the inn where I found the captain, and he asked me how I had fared. As I was relating my sorrows, he put his hand into his sleeve, and took out the purse with the sixty ducats, and gave it to me, saying: "I took this purse that you might know the want which the loss of the money would cause you, and that you might see how to remedy the loss." We started again with great joy, and went to Murcia, where our roads separated, and we parted after resting for eight days.

## III.

### OF WHAT HAPPENED TO ME IN BARCELONA.

I had letters from Don Juan Alonzo to the Archbishop of Saragossa, and from Don Hernando Enriquez de Ribera to the Admiral of Castille,[1] his first cousin; by whom I was very well received, and taken to kiss the hand of the King. News had just arrived that he had been elected Emperor. On another day I went to speak of my affairs to the King; the Duke of Bejar and the Admiral going with me, to pray that I might receive the habit of Santiago, and a place at court. The Emperor referred me to Don Garcia de Padilla of his council, who was a wrongheaded man. I said to him: "His majesty the Emperor has

---

[1] Don Fadrique Enriquez, Admiral of Castille, and third Count of Melgar, was a first cousin of King Ferdinand the Catholic; the King's mother, Juana, Queen of Aragon, having been a half sister of Alonzo de Enriquez, third Count of Melgar, and Admiral of Castille, who died in 1485. Don Fadrique was, in 1522, one of the Regents of the kingdom, during the rebellion of the Commons.

referred me to you, and I am well satisfied and give thanks
to God, because he has sent me to a knight and a learned
man, whose equal would not often be found. Your worship
must know that I have come to the Emperor, as to my natural King, that he may receive me in his court, like other
persons of good family whom he retains in his house, and
that he may give me the habit of Santiago. For I understand that the habit is conferred on gentle knights who may
conquer infidels, and I come well prepared to do so, and
well qualified by my descent, like the Admiral of Castille
and the Duke of Bejar. Your worship may be assured that
I am of gentle blood, and that I merit the habit of Santiago
for the services which I am prepared to render : and I beseech your worship to comply with my request, for I despise
labour, and dread poverty." He replied that he knew not
where I could go with a greater certainty of wasting my
labour and my money.

I gave him many thanks, and went to the Secretary
Francisco de los Cobos, giving him a letter from Don
Rodrigo Ponce de Leon, Count of Belen, in which he
stated who I was ; and saying the same as I had said to
Don Garcia. The Secretary told me that all the time I remained there would be lost, because the Emperor could not
receive me, and that I should spend all my money, going
from door to door soliciting favours. He added that I had
come at a very bad time, and advised me, before I spent
more money, to return home until a more opportune occasion offered ; reminding me that I must not suppose that I
could obtain what I wanted solely with the help of my long
descent, for that others, as well supplied with that article as
myself, spent many days in the same quest, with as little
success. I went away very much discontented with his
advice, and returned to Don Garcia, whom I followed about
for six months, hearing very soft and deceitful speeches,
such as he gave me on the first day. I spent all the money I

c

had in food for myself and my beasts and servants, until I was obliged to sell the former and dismiss the latter ; and at last I had nothing left but shoes and doublet, and was forced to take a pike and go to the wars. There was then a war against the Moors, and I passed through the streets of Barcelona, before the Emperor and his courtiers, among whom were some of my relations, in the ranks, with the other soldiers, carrying a pike on my shoulder. Two knights of my native town, the one named Francisco del Alcazar, and the other, Juan Melgarejo, when they saw me, came down to take me away; but I refused to go with them, and embarked as one of the soldiers.

---

## IV.

### OF WHAT HAPPENED TO ME IN THE EXPEDITION AGAINST THE MOORS.

We disembarked on an uninhabited island called Formentera, where we found the people whom we were to join from Barcelona, consisting of five thousand foot soldiers and four hundred men at arms, and three hundred light infantry, under the command of Diego de Vera, a veteran knight. In a few days we sailed for the island of Sicily, where we were joined by Don Diego de Monçada, prior of Messina, of the order of St. John, who was appointed captain-general of the army. He was quartered, with the cavalry, in a town called Trapani, and the infantry were encamped at a distance of four or five leagues, at a place called Marsala, with Diego de Vera as lieutenant-general. We were thus encamped for five months, during which time I will first tell you what happened to myself, and then what befell the army.

I, being of tender of age, though self-willed, having left my mother's house and come to a land of strangers, who shut their doors in my face, was taken very dangerously ill during two months. I had made no friends, because, during the voyage from Barcelona, I was so indignant and enraged at the treatment I had received, that I avoided every one. When I recovered, and had spent all my small supply of money, I desired to go to Marsala, where the infantry were encamped, to join the company of Captain Villaturiel. When I made as if I was going to pay for my lodging, the people, as I had made no complaint of my poverty, declined to receive payment, solely on account of my youth, and my weakness. I begged for food from door to door in the day time, but I fared very ill at night, as the people closed their doors early. In this manner I passed a month, when I began to collect faggots of wood and to sell them at a tavern, and in this way I passed another month. At last I fell in with a knight of Seville named Gonzalo Marino, captain and alcaide of Melilla for the Duke of Medina Sidonia, who came here to accompany the captain-general, Diego de Vera having command of the infantry, and Gonzalo Marino of the cavalry. This knight said that he was a friend of my father, and my fellow townsman, and he desired that I would honour him by using his person and his estate. He took me to his lodging, clothed me, and took me to the captain-general, speaking very highly of me, and after twelve days they gave me a company of infantry and made me a captain. Fifteen days afterwards the said Gonzalo Marino died, whom may God pardon, and soon afterwards the army set out, to drive the Moors from the island De los Gelves.[1]

## V.

### HOW THEY ATTACKED THE MOORS.

We sailed in a great fleet of ships, and with the same

[1] The modern island of Zerbi, on the African coast, between Tunis and Tripoli.

number of men as I have before stated, for though some had
died, yet others had arrived to take their places.  We were
delayed longer than we expected by calms and light winds.
On our arrival the Moors were prepared to receive us, numbering thirty thousand on foot, and thirty horsemen, there
being few horses on the island, and the Moors not having
had any opportunity of obtaining them.  We jumped on
shore, and, forming an encampment near the beach, passed
the night there.  Next day we began our march, in order
of battle, with great confidence and certainty of success,
which was the cause of all our misfortunes; for having
marched two leagues without meeting any enemy, we began
to think that there was no danger.  We then advanced without any caution, some picking figs and others dates, for the
country is thickly covered with palm trees, while others
entered the houses of the natives in search of plunder, but
only found a few jars of honey and raisins, which the people
had not had time to carry off.  We were in this state of disorder, when the Moors suddenly appeared, on all sides,
twenty thousand in front, five thousand in the rear, and
thirty horsemen on our flank, led by a Moor, dressed·like
one of our hermits and riding on a donkey.  Firm in their
false faith, they came on with such determination to die, that
I really believe they desired more to be killed themselves,
than to kill us; for they rushed upon our pikes with open
arms, as soon as they had hurled the stones and lances which
they held in their hands.  The said hermit and one thousand four hundred Moors were killed, and five hundred of
our people and seven hundred of the cavalry, which were
those who did not run away.  I escaped, though wounded,
with two or three others, the captain-general, and Diego de
Vera.  We assembled with great fear, because the advantages which we possessed in arms, were counterbalanced by
their knowledge of the country.  After we had rallied, we
again embarked, and sailed to an uninhabited island called

Favignana, two or three leagues from Trapani, on the coast of Sicily, where we were dismissed.[1]

[1] The island of *Los Gelves* is the modern island of Zerbi, on the coast of Africa, between Tunis and Tripoli. In 1497 the Sheikh of Los Gelves, having quarrelled with the King of Tunis, delivered the island into the hands of the Spaniards, and it was garrisoned by the Viceroy of Sicily.

Don Garcia de Toledo, in 1510, sailed with a fleet from Malaga, and seven thousand men. He was accompanied by Diego de Vera, and with sixteen vessels joined the Count Pedro Navarro, off Tripoli. Zerbi was their destination, a low sandy island, covered with palm trees and olives, and so close to the main land that in one place a man can pass over by a bridge. It has little water, and there are no towns, only a few scattered huts. It belonged to the King of Tunis, but was actually ruled by a Sheikh of its own.

The fleet arrived at Zerbi on August 8th, 1510, and the army landed without opposition. It was divided into seven squadrons, and Don Garcia marched in front with his knights. The Sheikh had one hundred and fifty cavalry and two thousand infantry badly armed. The troops began to march in the afternoon, but the heat was so great, and the dust from the sand so thick, that it was like walking through flames. They had scarcely gone two leagues when some began to fall from sheer thirst, and all suffered terribly. The van reached some palm groves, and hearing there were wells near some huts, they fell into disorder, and ran in search of water. The Moors took this opportunity to attack them. Some wished to retreat, but Don Garcia cried out that he did not come there to show his back, he seized a pike from an Aragonese and rushed upon the Moors, but his men fled, and Don Garcia with other captains were killed. The Count Navarro was one of the first to embark. Four thousand men were killed or taken prisoners. The Sheikh preserved the body of Don Garcia, and wrote to Don Diego de Monçada, the Viceroy of Italy, to offer it to him. Don Garcia was grandson of the first Duke of Alva.

In 1520 Don Diego de Monçada was again sent against the island of Zerbi, to root out a nest of pirates. Having disembarked his troops, he began the march, leaving Diego de Vera with a body of reserves. After a sharp encounter Monçada defeated the Moors; but Diego de Vera was suddenly attacked by a body of the enemy, who were in ambuscade, and his men were panic struck. In vain he tried to rally them, they fled, and he sent in haste to Monçada for succour, retreating to his ships with some loss. On the return of Monçada the fight was renewed, which was bloody and obstinate, but finally the Moors were put to flight. Monçada was wounded in the shoulder. The Sheikh then asked for peace, which was agreed to on condition that he should become

## VI.

### WHAT HAPPENED TO ME AFTERWARDS.

I went with three servants and a hundred ducats to the city of Palermo, where I passed two months enjoying myself, resting, and curing my wound, until I had spent nearly all my money, and was obliged to dismiss my servants. I then went to Messina, another city in the island of Sicily, and spent all that was left of my hundred ducats, while I was waiting for a passage to Naples. In order to avoid greater sins I became a ruffian, and, passing one day by a place where there were some women, I made love to one of them, and carried her off to Calabria. We went to a place called Reggio, but after nine or ten days the first lover of my mistress came in search of us, and, more by force than by fair means, he took her from me. In truth, both on account of my soul and my honour, I feared death in such a quarrel, more than the shame of a disgraceful defeat. I then went to Naples with eight ducats, which were obtained more through the cunning that my want had taught me, than by the force of my right arm.

## VII.

### OF WHAT HAPPENED TO ME IN NAPLES.

I arrived without linen or money, and dressed in rags, but I was known to many who had served in the same army, and who remembered that I had been a captain, which is considered a very honourable position in Italy, where those who have held that rank are always treated with respect and

a tributary to the King of Spain, and pay twelve thousand *escudos* a year, and that he should not allow any pirate or corsair to enter his ports. Monçada then returned to Sicily. *Mariana*, vi, p. 386 ; vii, p. 188 ; viii, p. 41.

consideration. I went straight to an inn in the street of Santa Catalina, where a servant saw me, who was employed by a knight in the household of the Viceroy, Don Ramon de Cardona, who came from my native place, and was named Don Alvaro Peres de Guzman. This gentleman, having more honour than money, sent word respecting my condition to the Marquis of       ,[1] who was very hospitable to strangers, and especially to those who bore his wife's name, which was Enriquez. Accordingly, while I was playing at cards, some gentlemen came in and cried out that I was a prisoner. Not knowing them by sight, I believed it, and ran to jump out of the window, thinking that it was because I had been a ruffian. One of the gentlemen was the Marquis himself, who said: "Sir, I am the alguazil who comes to arrest you, by order of Don Alonzo Perez de Guzman, who is also present; and, as a punishment for having gone to an inn when you had friends and relations in the city, you must go to prison, which is my house, and though the life which we shall lead you will be that of a prisoner, it will only last as long as your own will, and until you are rested." They then put me on a mule, and took me to the house of the Marquis, where I was as well received by the lady his wife as by her husband. Among many other kindnesses, they gave me a bed hung with velvet and gold embroidery to sleep in, and in the morning, though I slept till late owing to the good bed, when I awoke a servant brought in a tradesman with many pieces of brocade and silk, and velvet cloth, who measured me for a cloak and doublet, and other clothes, which were not a little needed. I remained here sixty days, and was very kindly treated; and at the end of that time I started for Rome, against the wish of my host, who gave me a hundred ducats, a beautiful white horse, another for my page, a trunk full of white linen, and thirteen yards of brocade well concealed amongst the shirts.

[1] Illegible in the MS.

## VIII.

On arriving at Rome I went to see the city, both inside and out, and then sought out one Juan de Ocampo, who was my countryman and relation, and who was delighted to see and be able to serve me. He directed me to go to another countryman, who was very rich and highly respected in Rome, named Garcia de Gibraleon. He received me in his house, and lodged me and my servants and beasts very hospitably for thirty days. I then set out for Germany, where I had heard that the emperor was going to be crowned. I started on a hack, with my page on another hack, and fifty ducats in money, and went to Bologna, where my page was taken ill. Here I remained, watching and attending upon him as his services deserved, until he died, and I had spent so much that I could not afford to hire another servant; so I sold the page's hack, and set out alone, without knowing Latin or any other language except my own, which is the one least understood in those parts. I first went to Mantua, thence to Florence, where I found them making a hundred silken hats for the Marquis of Tarifa, thence to Esplug, thence to Spires, thence to Augsburg, and thence to Cologne, where the King was. During this time, from the city of Bologna to Cologne, I passed through many dangers, suffering from hunger, thirst, and fatigue, as well as from solitude, losing my way, and going a hundred and fifty leagues, instead of fifty, from not being able to ask the road. When I was sixty leagues from Bologna I asked the way to Cologne, and they showed me a road which took me back to Bologna. Having no money, and not being able to ask for anything, I often suffered from the want of something to eat and drink, and I arrived in the city of Cologne half-starved and on foot.

On reaching Cologne I went straight to the Emperor, dressed in a grey doublet and cloak lined with fox skin, with a sword and dagger, and said : " Sire, I am one who, in Barcelona, being of gentle birth, and assisted by the Archbishop of Saragossa and the Admiral of Castille, petitioned your Majesty for the habit of Santiago, and, as I had done nothing to deserve it, your Majesty did not give it to me. Now I do deserve it, as you will see by this letter from the captain-general, whom you sent to attack the Moors. I beseech you to consider my services, my merit, my labour, and the length of the road by which I have come, and to reward me, and put me under an obligation to do more service." He took the letter and sent me to the Bishop of Badajos, who was afterwards Bishop of Palencia and Burgos, whose name was the Bachiller Mota. This priest gave me quicker despatch than I had given to the Moors, for he not only refused the habit of Santiago, but his people also kept the ten ducats with which I had come, for which I not only asked, but continued for ten days to try to get another audience of this Bishop or of the Emperor, until at last I was driven from their doors by force. What with the Emperor refusing to hear me, and the Bishop telling me to go about my business in the name of God, I was there for thirty days.

All this time I was often without anything to eat, and sometimes I went to the taverns and stole food, or stood in the streets and begged for the love of God. At last I fell in with Don Luis de Guzman, son of Don Rodrigo de Guzman, Lord of Algaba, a league from Seville, who was the cause of all my good luck, and all my honours.

He was grieved to see me in such a plight, and it is due to him that my soul was not utterly dishonoured and lost; for if his virtue and goodness had not led him to succour me, I should have ceased to have any confidence in the mercy of God, any more than in that of men, and if his love had not been excessive, I should neither have done what he

D

told me, nor would he have done so much for me. He took me to his lodging, where I found his two brothers, the one named Don Pedro de Guzman, and the other Don Rodrigo de Guzman, in whom I found as much kindness as in Don Luis, and they received me as if I had been their own brother arrived from the land of the Moors. They are so respected in Seville that, when they raised their caps the height of two fingers in saluting me, I took mine off, and bowed to the ground. They gave me clothes, placed me in the saddles of their mules while they sat on the crupper, and shared their beds with me. They gained me so much reputation that I found myself like one of themselves. The Commander of Alcantara, son of the Duke of Alva, who was at Cologne, was a cousin and great friend of these knights, and in order to please them, and filled with pity at the account they had given of me, he showed me much favour; while these excellent and charitable knights, from the time that they received me into their company, treated me with unbounded kindness. Their servants were ordered to attend upon me as if I had been one of themselves; they treated me as a brother; and I not only benefited by the impression which their high breeding made on me, but also by their example of love and gentleness, for what one thought the other desired, and what one desired the other thought. I never saw any disagreement among them, nor heard a single angry word in the five years that I was in their company, and lived at their expense. I never found in one more love than in another, so that I know not to which of them I am most obliged, nor which of them was the best. They were such good Christians, as well as knights, that, from having been intimate with them, I have hopes of being one whom it will please God to receive into glory.[1] The Commander

[1] These three brothers were descended from Juan Gudiel, alguazil mayor of Toledo, who married Dona Maria Ramirez de Guzman. The son of this marriage was Don Luis Gonzalez de Guzman, who was

of Alcantara got me an appointment from the Emperor, and I began to serve in the army. His Majesty went to Valenciennes, and the King of France marched against him with a great army. It seemed good to the Emperor and his Councillors to undertake other enterprizes, and I remained with the garrison, in the town of Valenciennes. It is a very large place, but in Flanders they are not called cities but towns. The Count of Nassau, with four or five thousand German infantry and some cavalry remained at Valenciennes, with the Commander of Alcantara, and other honourable Spanish knights.

## IX.

### OF WHAT HAPPENED AT VALENCIENNES.

Early one morning there was a call to arms, and we marched out of the camp. It turned out that the King of

elected grand master of Calatrava in 1407, and was captain general of Jaen and Cordova, where he had many hard fights with the Moors of Granada. In 1431 he was with the army of King John II on the Vega of Granada. His son, Juan de Guzman, was the first Lord of Algaba, about a league from Seville. His son, Luis de Guzman, Lord of Algaba, married Ynez Ponce de Leon, daughter of the Count of Arcos ; and his son, Roderigo de Guzman, Lord of Algaba, married Leonora, daughter of Lope Vasquez de Acuña, second Count of Buendia, by Ynez Enriquez, daughter of the second Admiral of Castille of the Enriquez family.

Rodrigo de Guzman and Leonora Vasquez de Acuña were the parents of the three brothers, Luis, Rodrigo, and Pedro. There was another brother, Diego, and two sisters. Luis, the eldest brother, married Leonora de Manrique, daughter of the third Count of Paredes, by whom he had a son Francisco, who was created Marquis of Algaba.

Leonora, wife of the eldest brother Luis, was daughter of the third Count of Paredes, son of Pedro Manrique the second Count, who was brother of Jorge, the famous author of the *Coplas de Manrique*, and son of Rodrigo de Manrique, first Count of Paredes, created in the last year of King John II. He gained many victories over the Moors, and captured the city of Huesca, in Granada.

France, with the largest army that he had assembled since
his accession, was approaching. We marched in great haste
to oppose the passage of a river which was two leagues from
Valenciennes; but they were before us, and half their army
had already crossed. We believed that they were not in
great force, while they thought that we were, and we opened
fire upon them with five or six pieces of artillery. They
awaited our approach, and our captain-general fell back.[1]
The Emperor and the Count of Nassau had retired, and
we followed them to Tournay, a great town in Flanders,
which was besieged by Monsieur de Fresnes. The Count
of Nassau spoke to the Emperor respecting my services, and
he at last gave me the habit of Santiago; but before I received it, I challenged a knight on account of certain expressions, for which offence I was confined in the house of
Don Alvaro de Luna, who treated and fed me very well
for two months, during which time I was his prisoner, and
his wife, Dona Catalina Valori, showed me much kindness.
I shall not relate the cause of the challenge, nor how it
ended, because it would be prejudicial to a third person.
I was in prison until the Emperor sailed for Spain, when I
was taken in a ship to the port of Santander, still under
arrest. My sentence was then declared, which was very
cruel; for the Emperor was enraged, saying that I had
broken my word. The Emperor sent for me and abused me
because I had said certain things against a knight, to the
ladies of his court, which were found afterwards to be lies.
He sneered at me, and said: " You said so and so, and such
an one says that it was not so." I replied that I challenged
the man for two reasons, one, because what I said was true;
and the other, because, even if it had been a lie, as I had

[1] This was in 1521. Robertson says : " In the neighbourhood of
Valenciennes, through an excess of caution, an error with which he
cannot be often charged, Francis lost an opportunity of cutting off the
whole imperial army."—*Works*, v, p. 180.

said it with my mouth, I would make it true with my arm. I was sentenced to four years of banishment from the dominions of the Emperor, and to serve in an outpost of the Moorish frontier, called Melilla, and the grant of the habit of Santiago, as well as that of two hundred ducats, were revoked. The Emperor then dismissed me, both from his household and his muster roll, and I went to Seville, for it was five years since I had been there, and when I set out I was but recently married.

## X.

### HOW I SET OUT FROM SEVILLE, TO GO INTO BANISHMENT.

When I left Seville, I dressed two pages and a running foot boy in black doublets, with initials of green velvet on their shoulders, and breasts, and two badges, with a globe and a sword run through it, worked on them, in place of the arms of my fathers, which I inherited, and which are lions and castles, and pots, and serpents' mouths.[1] From the globe there came out four scrolls, on which were written *Fortune* (Ventura), and on a border round the badges was also worked the word *Fortune*. I set out with a hundred

---

[1] These were the arms of the Guzmans, Dukes of Medina Sidonia, which Don Alonzo bore by right of his great grandmother, Beatriz de Guzman, sister of the first Duke of Medina Sidonia. They were : Party per saltire, first and third, on a field *azure*, a caldron checky, *or* and *gules*, with three serpents' heads on each side of the handle ; second and fourth, five ermines *sable* on a field *argent ;* an orle of castles and lions of the royal colours of Spain. The orle was added to the arms of the first Count of Niebla, grandfather of the first Duke of Medina Sidonia, on his creation in 1371 by King Henry II, when he married that sovereign's daughter Beatriz.

Our young friend's paternal arms of Enriquez, were those of the Counts of Gijon y Noroña, granted in 1373. Quarterly, on the upper part two lions rampant *purpure* on a field *argent*, on the lower part a castle *or* on a field *gules*, on an orle *or*, eight cheques *azure* and *argent*.

ducats in money, and my person well supplied both with
clothing and arms; and went first to Malaga, where an
order had arrived from the Emperor, on account of a request
from the prior of St. John, as follows:

" THE KING,

" Don Alonzo Enriquez de Guzman, on account of a duel
which you fought with Don Francisco de Mendoza, alcalde
in our court, we banished you from our realms for four
years, and we ordered you to serve on the frontier of
Melilla. Now the prior of St. John, Don Diego de Toledo,[1]
has besought us to grant you permission to go with him to
the city of Rhodes, which is besieged by infidels; and we,
for the service of God, grant you permission to reside in the
said city of Rhodes for the said four years; given in this
our town of Valladolid."[2]

The prior wrote to me to say that he would wait for me
at Carthagena, to which place I went, but he was already
gone. I then proceeded to Alicante, where I found a ship
owned by Venetians, about to sail for Sicily, to which place
the prior had directed me to follow him.

XI.

WHAT HAPPENED TO ME IN ALICANTE, AND ON BOARD THE VENETIAN
SHIP.

I was twenty-two days in Alicante, waiting until the load-
ing of the ship was completed, and I passed this time like a
man full of sorrow and despair. It caused me grief to think
how many labours and dangers I had undergone, and how

[1] A younger son of Don Fadrique de Toledo, second Duke of Alva.
[2] Sultan Solyman commenced the siege of Rhodes in July 1522, and
the Grand Master L'Isle Adam finally evacuated the island, with his
Knights of St. John, on January 1st, 1523.

soon I had lost all that I had obtained with so much trouble.
I thought how I had lost the habit of Santiago and the
favour of the Emperor ; and how I must recover all by my
own hard work, for I had left no one at court who grieved
for me. It appeared to me that I must perform terrible
deeds in order that they might come to the ears of the Emperor, and thus be the cause of recovering my position ; for
when men have friends and relations at the Emperor's side,
any small affair is magnified into a great service, while important service done by the friendless is turned into a trifle.
With these thoughts I went on board the ship, when she
was ready for sea, and, as I always carried myself as a man
of consequence, I had a cabin prepared, with provisions
more than sufficient for myself, for my servants, and for four
other men who had made their appearance, passing themselves off as soldiers bound for Italy.

At this time there were orders to search in all parts, and
especially in the ports of the kingdom, by command of the
Emperor, for one Captain Martin, who had been the principal cause of all the insurrections and disturbances in the
kingdom of Valencia, where many virgins and nuns had
been violated, widows abused, and many other enormities
perpetrated, too numerous to recount. At about eleven
o'clock of the night on which I had embarked, the Governor
of Alicante came on board with a number of followers. He
is a very honourable knight, of good lineage, and so excellent himself, that to be descended from him would be sufficient for his successors, without any more remote ancestry.
As soon as he came on board he inquired for me, although
we had never before exchanged a word in our lives, and
went down into my cabin. He then said : " I have received
an order from the Emperor to detain the persons of certain
evil doers and their servants, but it cannot apply to so good
a knight as your worship." I then kissed his hand with the
most respectful speeches I could make, and he caused the

said order of the Emperor to be shown to me, which filled
me with fear ; for I believed that any other Governor, if he
had found this Captain Martin on board, would also have arrested me and put me to death, for being in the same ship
with him.    At that moment the alguazils who had been
searching the ship, reported that they had not found the
fugitive.

Next morning, at dawn, we got under weigh with the
wind on the beam, as the sailors say, which is as good for
going as for returning, because it blows on the side of the
ship, and it is only necessary to know how to set the sails.
When we were about ten leagues from the land, I being on
deck half sea sick, and talking to the four comrades who
were going to Italy as soldiers, the said malefactor, Captain Martin, came up, very wet with wine, because up to
this time he had been concealed in a half-empty barrel.
He gave thanks to God for his escape, when he ought
rather to have given them to me, and saluted me and all
who stood round him, with great exultation.    He informed
me, as I already knew, that it was he whom the Governor,
Don Pedro Masa, had come to arrest.

I then considered that the Emperor had issued the order
which the Governor had shown me, and that if I did not
perform some strange and terrible deed I should neither be
heard of nor taken into favour ; so I resolved to arrest the
fugitive, though I well knew that it would be a desperate
undertaking.    I, therefore, determined to begin by cunning,
and I protested to the captain, with a great oath, that the
Emperor had sent me, at the request of my relations, to
assemble five thousand men in Sicily to relieve Rhodes,
which was besieged by the Turk with all his power ; but
that I had left the Emperor's commission at my inn, through
forgetfulness.    I besought him to reflect how God and the
Emperor would be served by this work ; and that I should
lose the chance of leading the expedition, which was my

first command, owing to this want of care. I then offered him three hundred ducats if he would return. He replied that he was sorry for my misfortune, but that there was no help for it, because the merchants who had their goods on board would not consent to return; and even if they did consent, and he returned to the port, that in this season he might be detained a month, during which time he would have to feed himself and his crew. "Though I cannot help you," he concluded, "I can give you a piece of advice. The distance from here to Majorca is ten leagues, I will put you on shore there, and you can then return to Alicante in a boat in a very short time." When I saw that he was determined, I returned him many thanks for his advice, and waited until every one went down to dinner, except the pilot, who steered the ship, two of my servants, and the four comrades who were passengers, named Ochoa, Oviedo, Ortiz, and Bartolomé. I then called them all to me, except the pilot, and made exactly the same speech to them as I had just made to the captain, concluding with a proposal that we should take the vessel by force of arms, and entreating them to assist me. I determined to flatter them by giving them the title of captains, and said: "You, Captain Ortiz, go forward and haul the fore sail over to windward; and you, Captain Oviedo, approach the pilot and kill him if he raises his voice; and you, Captain Ochoa, guard this side of the vessel, and prevent any one from coming up the hatchway." Bartolomé, who had at first refused to join us, was now in a great fright because I did not call him captain also; so I said to him: "You, Captain Bartolomé, guard the other side of the vessel." I then, with my two servants, our party numbering seven in all, went straight to the main mast, drew my sword, and cut away the halliards, which were belayed to a cleat at the foot of the mast. The main sail came down so suddenly that I had no time to run from under it, and it threw me down, bruising my head

E

a little against the deck. On hearing the noise, all the
people who were at dinner jumped up from the table, and
the captain put his head up through a small scuttle near the
main mast. As soon as I saw the head I ran my sword at
it, a little below the eye, so the captain fell dead ; and I
myself did not feel very lively, as my fall had half stunned
me, and my bruise was bleeding a good deal. The pilot
joined us, though not with the same view, as he believed
that I intended to seize the ship, in order to turn corsair ;
and he put the helm down, which was what I wanted.
When the people came up from the cabin they fought so
fiercely that three of my captains were killed, among whom
was Captain Bartolomé, who fought like a lion. Of the
other side nineteen were killed and wounded, with a piece
of artillery which was on deck. The people of Alicante
armed two brigantines and many boats, and came out to us,
some thinking that the ship was on fire, and others that she
was sinking, and that we were signalling for assistance by
means of the piece of artillery, as is the usual custom. They
came out with as much speed as possible, and the Governor,
Don Pedro Masa, with them. The men of the other party
had been driven below, but if the assistance had come a little
later, I should have fainted from loss of blood caused by a
very bad lance wound in the thigh, for the men below had
broken up several planks in the deck, whence they attacked
us. We gladly helped the people up the side, and Don
Pedro Masa came up to me with a drawn sword in one
hand, and a staff of justice in the other, and ordered me to
give up my sword in the King's name. I gave it up with
great pleasure, for I was very tired, and presently I felt
faint, until they gave me some wine and bled me. The
people then came up from below, and among them was
Captain Martin, dressed as a sailor, and thinking that he
would not be recognized. But I, who had braved so many
dangers on his account, did not fail to recognize him, and

when Don Pedro Masa asked, where is this gentleman? I answered by asking if a notary was present. They said there were five, and I replied that they would bear witness that I had delivered this Captain Martin into the hands of Don Pedro Masa, Governor of Alicante and Orihuela. He was then arrested.

The Governor took me to his house, and treated me with great kindness. Next morning five of the men who had concealed Captain Martin were put to death, and an express was sent to the Emperor, with a letter informing him of the good news, and speaking so strongly in my favour, that my judgment fails me in giving expression to the good which was done me by the clerk who wrote it, and the paper, and the ink, employed by that most honourable knight, Don Pedro Masa.

## XII.

### WHAT THE EMPEROR SAID IN REPLY TO THE DISPATCH OF THE GOVERNOR, AND WHAT HAPPENED AFTERWARDS.

The Emperor replied by thanking the Governor for his care and diligence in having captured this Captain Martin, and saying that his report of Don Alonzo Enriquez confirmed what he had always hoped from his disposition. He gave orders that the said Captain Martin should presently be sent to the city of Valencia, where he had commenced his treasonable practices, and delivered up to the Viceroy; and that the said Don Alonzo should have charge of him, adding that he who had understood so well how to capture him, would be well able to guard him. He also wrote to the Viceroy of Valencia, both regarding Don Alonzo and the said Captain Martin.

The Governor of Alicante then provided me with a litter,

because I was not yet recovered from my wound, and an escort, consisting of ten horsemen and a dozen crossbow men on foot, and everything I could require on the journey. All Valencia came out to meet me, and I delivered my captain into the hands of the authorities, who placed him in a very strong prison, and after three days sentenced him to death. He besought the justices that, as he was a Biscayan, they would send a priest to confess him who spoke his language, and would be able to understand him. This request appeared reasonable, and, as Valencia is a city where all sorts of people congregate, they found a Biscayan priest who happened to be a relation of Captain Martin, although they did not know it until afterwards. The priest went into the prison, and came out protesting and swearing that it was impossible that justice could be done on that day, because Captain Martin knew many important secrets bearing on the King's service. As he had been engaged in affairs of moment, the story was believed. The priest's conduct was afterwards more that of the relation than the confessor. He got permission to pass the night with the condemned, and, on pretence of going out to procure supper for both, he got a jar of vinegar and some iron tools, with which he made a hole from the prison into a narrow lane, through the wall, and neither the priest nor the captain ever appeared again.

## XIII.

### WHAT HAPPENED TO ME AFTERWARDS.

The Viceroy of Valencia sent for me, and said, on the part of the Emperor, that his Majesty had given orders that, as I could do such good service against his enemies, I was to go to Molverde,[1] which is four leagues from Valencia, and

---

[1] This must be Murviedro, on the site of the ancient Saguntum. It was formerly a port, but now the sea has receded for more than a league.

take command of five hundred men who were quartered there, to re-establish order in the island of Majorca. This island was in rebellion against the King's service, and I was ordered to join the Viceroy, Don Miguel de Urrea, whom I should find there with ten thousand men, together with Don Juan de Velasco, the captain-general of the galleys, who was there with a large fleet. I went to take command of the five hundred men, but as soon as they saw that I only brought one month's pay with me, when they had demanded five, they mutinied and agreed to go to Fuentarabia, where the Emperor had an army opposing the French. I went to tell the Viceroy of Valencia, and he ordered me to go to the Duke of Soborba, who was in Soborba,[1] by which place the mutineers would have to pass. He also sent me a letter to the Duke, ordering him, in the King's name, to do what I might require, and to speak to my men and induce them to embark by fair means ; but, if they refused, to use force, because there was great want of men in Majorca, and none in Fuentarabia. I took the post, and found the Duke in a country house, half a league from Soborba, hearing mass. As soon as I arrived I gave him the letter of the Viceroy, but he did not want to read it until mass was over ; so I urged him strongly, because by this time the soldiers were very near. At first he treated me like a postman, but when he had read the letter he apologized, and asked what it was that he was expected to do. I replied that his lordship ought to go out, and explain to the soldiers, with fair words, that it would be a great service to his Majesty to reinforce the Viceroy of Majorca, and reduce the people to obedience, while there was no occasion to march to Fuentarabia. The Duke replied : " Do not ask me to do such a thing, my good sir. The King cannot desire that I should die like a fool.

---

[1] Probably Segorbe, near Valencia, and beyond Murviedro, in a very fertile valley. There never was a Duke of Segorbe or Soborba, but the Duke of Medina Celi had a house there.

I know soldiers very well; that many together have many
spectacles, that they are the sons of many mothers, that if
one throws a stone they will all follow his example, and if
one begins to call names, they are all abusive. But, if you
desire it, I will get out two thousand men and ten pieces of
artillery, and then if they will not obey, I will force them
on board the ships, dead or alive." I replied that I did not
think there would be time for these preparations, because
the men had already reached the olive yard, which is only
half a league from Soborba. He then told me that he knew
his duty as well as I could tell it him, and that he would be
amongst the men in less than half an hour; and he called his
secretary to be in attendance, mounted a mule, took me up
behind him, and, waving his hat, rode off towards Soborba,
calling on every man to follow him. As we rode along, the
labourers left their ploughs, and the diggers their spades,
and trained on behind us, so that we were followed by more
than a hundred men before we reached Soborba. From
Soborba we set out with four pieces of artillery, and two
thousand men, some on foot and others on horseback. Presently two envoys came on the part of the soldiers, and,
throwing themselves on their knees on the ground, one of
them said : " Most puissant lord, we come on the part of
five hundred foot soldiers, our companions, to beseech your
mighty lordship to give us victuals for to-day, and permission to pass through your domain ; for we go, in the service
of the Emperor, to join his army which is now before Fuentarabia." The Duke replied that their Captain, Don Alonzo
Enriquez, was present, and I ordered them to be seized and
lodged in prison. We then sent a volley from the cross
bows at the soldiers, and we saw them, in order of battle,
with the matches lighted, showing a great desire to fight.
But they sent two other envoys, who said the same thing.
The Duke asked permission from me, in their presence, to
speak to them, and I replied that his lordship could do as

he thought fit. He then said : " Most loyal Spaniards, I deeply regret that you should have commenced to act in a way which your ancestors would never have thought of, and I entreat you to return to your companions, and to tell them that, as well for the sake of their loyalty as for my love, they must embark." They replied that they would repeat his words, and that they kissed his most illustrious hands. While they were returning to their companions a messenger arrived from the Viceroy of Valencia with a letter informing me that a man, who called himself Captain Alonzo, was at the head of the mutineers, and directing me to have him hanged. Soon afterwards six more of the soldiers presented themselves, among whom was this Captain Alonzo, and they said many things to the Duke, protesting that five months pay was owing to them, and that they had only received one ; that they were ordered to embark to sail for an island where there was pestilence and famine, and which was a grave for soldiers ; and that they did not wish to die so miserably. The Duke turned to me and said : " Don Alonzo, order that I am to act as your alguazil." He then said to one of the soldiers : " Are not you he whom they called Captain Alonzo ?" The man replied that he was, and the Duke caused him to be hanged. He then sent a messenger to the Viceroy, requesting him to give the men two months pay, to which he consented. Next day, in the evening, I marched the soldiers down to the port, and on the following morning we went on board, and made sail.

## XIV.

### WHAT HAPPENED TO ME AT MAJORCA.

At early dawn on Wednesday morning I left the port with the said five hundred soldiers, and a supply of provisions,

to join the army at Majorca, in nine vessels. A smaller number
would easily have contained us, but we wished the enemy to
think that our force was more numerous than it really was,
as well as to encourage and console our friends. We arrived
off the city, at night fall, and found the army of the Emperor encamped. A galley was sent out to reconnoitre us,
and as soon as we were known, they saluted us with artillery, and we were very well received. The Viceroy and
Captain-General of Majorca soon afterwards proclaimed that
five thousand men had arrived, under Don Alonzo Enriquez,
a relation of the Emperor. On the following day, by agreement, the captain of the city, who was called Captain Crispin, a cap maker (married forcibly to a lady who had been
the wife of one of the principal gentlemen of the place), with
fifty men as guards, came out and sought speech with me.
The Viceroy sent me to hear him, telling me of many
great enormities which he had committed, such as violating
maidens the daughters of knights, butchering boys like
sheep at the shambles, burying them in the earth with their
heads out, to use as quoit pins, and other atrocities of a
similar nature. The excuse he made was that, if it was not
for him, the people would commit still worse excesses, and
that he permitted them to do these things, because if he
opposed them, they would kill him. When I asked him
why he had driven out the Viceroy, who represented the
person of the King, he answered that the Viceroy had committed many acts of injustice, and that when the people had
complained of them by letters and messages to the Emperor, he had transmitted their complaints to the Council of
Aragon, where the Viceroy had brothers-in-law and relations who reported to the Emperor in the Viceroy's favour,
and against the people. They had, therefore, resolved to
oblige the Emperor to hear them, by expelling the Viceroy;
they assured me that they desired nothing but justice, and
that if I wanted to take the city with the troops which fol-

lowed me, they would deliver it up, on condition that they should receive pardon, and that the King should send them another Viceroy.

I replied that they asked for things which I had not the power to grant, and that the Emperor had sent me to obey the orders of the Viceroy.

Crispin answered (who, as I have before said, was their captain) : " We beseech you to mediate between us and the Viceroy, and to induce him to consent to a deputation being sent to the King, two sent by him and one by the people, that his Majesty may hear us ; and, during the time that the deputies are going and coming, you shall remain in the city with thirty soldiers, and I will deliver the city to whomsoever the King may command, even if it should be the said Don Miguel de Urrea."

Having agreed to this, I entered the city, and the deputies set out. After twenty-seven days they returned, and said that the Emperor had listened to them every day for two hours, during eight days, and they returned very well satisfied. Nine days afterwards an order arrived, which the Viceroy sent to me, together with another of his own, and they gave them to me through the closed doors. The tenor of these orders was as follows. Here is that of the Emperor :

## " THE KING.

" Don Alonzo Enriquez de Guzman, our Captain, you have kept the word which you gave to the people of the city of Majorca, and I have heard them, because they besought me. I now desire you to obey the orders of the Viceroy, Don Miguel de Urrea."

That of the Viceroy was as follows :

" Magnificent and noble Don Alonzo Enriquez de Guzman, his Majesty's Captain in this our army, I, Don Miguel de Urrea, Viceroy of this kingdom of Majorca for his sacred Catholic Majesty, order you to seize the person of Crispin the

F

cap maker, commonly called Captain Crispin, and those of
the thirteen members of his Council; and I desire you to
open the gates of the city at four o'clock this afternoon; and
if the people will not permit you to do so, I command you
to come forth, that I may avail myself of your advice."

They delivered these orders to me at ten o'clock in the
morning. I then went to the *plaza*, where I found Captain
Crispin with his guards and five of his Councillors. I told
them that I had received orders to deliver up the city to
Don Miguel de Urrea, and that I trusted more to their good
faith than to my force, for that I had only thirty men, while
they had thirty thousand. I reminded them that they had
promised to let me go, and advised them to respect their
words, and thus place me under an obligation, and give
evidence to the Emperor that they were honest men.

Crispin answered: " Sir, you have spoken as a good
knight should, and I declare that I will be the first to obey
the orders of his Majesty." The rest all said the same, so
I went to dinner, and each man departed to his own house.
After dinner I called an assembly, and ordered none of the
men to bring their arms. I then, with many kind words,
put the Captain and his Councillors in irons, and formed a
solemn procession, with all the women and children bare
footed on one side, and the men bare footed on the other.
Then, with loud cries for mercy, they went to the gates of
the city, where an altar surmounted by a crucifix was set up.
Here we met the Viceroy, with Don Juan de Velasco, captain-general of the galleys, on his left hand. I then delivered up the keys of the city to him, and said : " The gates
are now open, and the desires of the people are turned to
serve the King and your Lordship, they seek for pardon,
and bring the heavenly Advocate to intercede for them."
He did not answer me, but took me by the arm, while the
priest began to say the " *Gloria in excelsis Deo.*" The
Viceroy then entered the city, and cut into four quarters

the said Captain Crispin, his thirteen Councillors, and an alguazil, and visited the rest with justice. The number of persons who were hung and quartered was four hundred and twenty.[1]

The Viceroy wrote very favourably of my services, to the Emperor, and his Majesty ordered me to go to Iviça, because news had arrived that the island was threatened by Barbaroja, King of Algiers.

## XV.

### HOW I WENT TO IVIÇA.

I received an order from the King, the tenour of which was as follows :

" THE KING.

" Don Alonzo Enriquez de Guzman, an officer in our household, and Captain in our army ; the Viceroy has written to inform us of the zeal and vigour with which you have done what was necessary. This has pleased us, and we would now have you to know that, by reason of a great pestilence, the number of the inhabitants of the island of Iviça has been greatly reduced, while there is a rumour that Barbaroja, the King of Algiers, is coming with a design to

---

[1] Mariana says that, in the middle of March 1521, the insurrection of the Commons of Valencia and Castille spread to the island of Majorca. The leader of the insurgents was a man of obscure birth named Juan Crispin. Following the example of the Valencians, the people of Majorca appointed thirteen Syndics to govern them, and drove out the Viceroy Don Miguel de Urrea. Thirty noble knights, who had taken refuge in the fort, were massacred, but others escaped to the town of Alcudia, at the east end of the island ; where they repulsed the attacks of the insurgents, with great slaughter, on two occasions. Palma, the capital of Majorca, was reduced, after a siege of three months, and the Viceroy re-entered the town on the 7th of March, 1522. *Mariana*, viii, lib. i, cap. x, p. 79 ; and lib. ii, cap. ii, p. 112.

conquer the said island. The people have petitioned that
we will succour and defend them, and we therefore entrust
the defence of the said island to you, and charge you presently to take five hundred men, and embark them in galleys
which Don Juan de Velasco, our captain-general, has been
ordered to provide, for the said island. We also direct you
to see that the soldiers treat the inhabitants well, and that
the inhabitants supply the soldiers with lodging, bread, and
salt ; and, as there is a pestilence and other dangers in the
island, we desire that, in event of your death, the next in
command shall become captain, and if he should die the
next, and may God give you health. Given in our town of
Valladolid. I, the King."

I showed this order to the soldiers, who, though fearful of
going to the island on account of the pestilence, yet did not
take it much amiss, because the pestilence was also raging on
the island of Majorca. We embarked in the galleys, and
came to the island of Iviça by the port which is most distant
from the city. This port is called *El puerto de Por-maña*,[1]
and consists of a church, and a strong tower called San
Antonio. We put into this port, because Don Juan Velasco,
the captain-general of the galleys, was in a great fright of
the pestilence, both because he was made of flesh and blood,
and possessed a good understanding ; and because he desired
to live to see the Emperor, and enjoy the relation of the
many deeds he had performed in battles by sea and land in
the island of Majorca. The Governor of the city, with the
other authorities, came to receive us, and Don Juan talked to
them from a great distance, taking care to keep them to
leeward, influenced by his fear of the pestilence. We agreed
that they should give me four ducats a day for my table,
and a hundred a month ; and for the soldiers, three for each
man, fifteen for the ensign, and ten for the serjeant. They

---

[1] Or Pormañy. The island of Iviça is divided into five *cuartones* or
districts, of which Pormañy is one.

willingly agreed to this, thinking it would not be necessary
to pay for more than a month, and knowing that they were
in great danger, as you will presently see.

I went, with all my people, with the people of the city,
while Don Juan predicted that I should certainly die, re-
peating his prophecy many times. After two days he sent
to me for forty musketeers, as some latteen rigged Moorish
vessels were in sight, which he desired to attack. The pestilence was now on board the galleys, and I dreaded going
on board, from fear of it. A captain was sent to bring me,
who said that Don Juan was ill, but he did not tell me of
what disease. When I arrived, however, it became known
to me that he was down with the pestilence, with a swelling
under the armpit, which is very dangerous. The first word
he said to me was : " Alonzo, my brother, I am seized !"
I replied : " Behold how our lives are in the hands of God
alone ; for I, who went into the midst of the pestilence, am
still in good health, and you, who were laughing at me, are
stricken. May it please God that your illness may be slight."

I then went out in chase of the Moorish vessels. We
fought with four of them, capturing one, and the approach
of night alone prevented us from taking the others. While
we were fighting on board the vessel which we afterwards
captured, Don Juan came out to help us, in his shirt, armed
with a sword and shield; and he fell down into the hold
amidships.[1] We returned into port, and I went to the city,
with my troops, and on the same night the said Don Juan
died of the pestilence. The galleys sailed, with his body, to
Denia, and thence to Carthagena, where he was buried.

I had been fifteen days on the island when nine large
Moorish vessels arrived at the port of Pormaña, which is
two leagues and a half from the city. The Moors and Turks
disembarked immediately. They numbered five hundred
men, all armed with muskets, and dressed in red doublets,

---

[1] They were, probably, half-decked vessels.

with five pieces of artillery. They commenced an attack on the church of San Antonio, which I have before said is near the port, where two friars, thirty women, and many peasants, who live in huts in the open country, had taken refuge. As soon as I received the news, I sallied forth from the city, resolved to die with the greatest pleasure, fighting in the service of God against those infidels. I had one hundred and fifty soldiers with me, being all that the pestilence had left of five hundred, of whom fifty were musketeers, and one hundred pikemen. I advanced until I was within half a league of the Moors, when I heard that they were entering the church; but they turned round to oppose me, when my forces came in sight. I then addressed the soldiers, as follows: "You know that only fifteen days ago we came to this island, and that, without fighting, three hundred and fifty of our number are dead, and have been deprived of the pleasure of doing what we are about to do in the service of God and of our King, defending those who are shut up in yonder church, and fighting the enemies of our holy Catholic faith. Remember how many have died since we were born, and how soon we must die, even if we lived in the most healthy land in the world; and therefore the greatest joy we can find will be to bathe ourselves in the blood of those infidels."

My ensign replied: "Sir, we now know that your lordship understands how to speak and to act, and you know that we can listen and work." They all declared that they were ready to venture the loss of little, and the chance of great gain; and we resumed our march. A soldier then took me aside, and said: "Sir, the great Captain of glorious memory always said that his chief duty was to listen to the soldiers, and, therefore, you ought not to fail in that duty. Now, though poor, I am desirous to serve the King and your lordship, and therefore I ought to be heard." I told him to let me know what he had got to say, and he proceeded. " I have now been in this profession of arms more than twenty-three years, and I have seen and heard many things. Our enemy numbers five hundred men, and we are one hundred. I do not remind you of this because I do not wish to fight as well as the rest, for I will fight as if I was one hundred men, but that you may not do a thing by which you can gain nothing. If you are defeated, you will lose your men, and the enemy will take the city which you are sent here to defend. We are badly armed, and dying of thirst, and hunger, for we have now marched two leagues." Thanking him for his good intentions, I replied : " I have listened to you, as you say that the great Captain was accustomed to do. You say that we are one hundred and the enemy five hundred. It is true ; but we are Christians, and they are Moors, and this is a sufficient answer to your objection. But you say that you are as good as a hundred men, the other soldiers number another hundred, which makes two hundred, and I will fight for three hundred more. Thus you see that the enemy has no advantage over us in point of numbers. If you are dying of hunger and thirst, I will give you a piece of bread ; but I thought that each man was carrying his own food, according to my orders, and at a short distance in front there is a place where you will be able to drink; besides, the Moors generally carry figs and raisins with them, which we can take." He replied : " Sir, I understand all this very well, but, according to the laws of war you ought not fight for two hours, in order that you may have time to rest your soldiers, and take up your position in yonder plain, where the battle must be fought. During that time I could go from here to the city for a pair of shoes, and return again, for, as you see, I have got none." As soon as I clearly saw that he was afraid, I wanted to stab him, but did not think that it would appear dignified, so I said : "Why do you prefer going two leagues for a pair of shoes, to entering the battle ?" He answered :

" Because I wish to die like a man, and not like a beast."
I then told him that if he said another word to me or to any
of the soldiers, I would have him hanged."

Having rested my troops, I formed them in order of
battle, and, happening to turn my head, I saw my soldier
running away towards the city, like a rabbit. I sent the
alguazil after him, on a horse, who caught him, and I then
caused him to be hanged on a fig tree, with the following
inscription fastened to his breast : " Don Alonzo ordered
this man to be hanged, because he had no shoes."

## XVI.

### HOW WE FARED IN THE BATTLE, AND HOW I CHALLENGE BARBAROJA.

The enemy now advanced against us, and their captain
was about ten paces in front, dressed in a robe reaching to
the ground, with a gilded musket and lighted match. I was
also about the same distance in front of my men, dressed in
white shoes, a doublet of white velvet, and a gilded corslet,
but with no other armour, so that they gave me seventeen
wounds below the waist and on my arms. I was armed with
a pike, and a sword in my girdle. My ensign, being a
valiant man, accompanied me, and for this reason he entrusted the standard to another trusty soldier, to be carried
in its proper place, which is nearly in the middle of the
squadron.

At the first encounter, when the Captain of the enemy
was going to fire his musket, I gave him a blow in the chest
with my pike, and my ensign, whose name was Morata the
One Eyed, gave him a blow with his pike on the right side,
which penetrated to his heart, so that he jumped high in the
air and fell dead. I then drew my sword, and the battle
began. They killed seventeen of our men, and wounded

me and many others; and we killed sixty of the Moors, and took forty prisoners, wounding many others. They then fled into the water up to their armpits, and got on board their vessels, sailing to an uninhabited island called Formentera, two leagues distant, where they remained for five days without a captain, and afterwards sailed for their own country.

After nineteen days ten galleys and five brigantines, belonging to the French, sailed from Marseilles, with the intention of capturing the city, for they had heard that it was badly garrisoned and in want of provisions. They sent a message to me to say that they were cruising after the Moors, and that they desired to come into port. I replied that there was an island called Formentera, two leagues distant, where the Moors were accustomed to resort, and that, if they wanted Moors, they would find them there, but that here there were only Christians and servants of the Emperor. As I had not yet recovered from my wounds, I treated with the Frenchmen from my bed, and I ordered the artillery to be fired at them, to which they did not fail to reply. One galley went to the bottom, and the others sailed away, news of which I sent to the Emperor.

A few days afterwards the Governor died, and, by virtue of the Emperor's letters and orders, I continued in command of the island. I was there for five more months, besides the four months during which I had only been a captain. But I enjoyed the former period much more than the time during which I was in authority as Governor of the island. I gained nothing but long skirts to my dress, for in real advantages and honours it profited me nothing. Formerly I could go about at night making love, and in the day time I could kill or grant life to any man, without having to give any account of my deeds; but, after I assumed this office of Governor, I could act, but always in the fear of my responsibility to the Emperor. After the lapse of five months the presence of

G

an armed force was no longer necessary, and I therefore wrote the following letter to his Majesty :

"His most Catholic Royal Majesty.

"By my servant, Francisco de Villalobos, I have written to your Majesty concerning certain things appertaining to your Majesty's service, and I beseech your Majesty to hear the said Francisco de Villalobos, and to grant my request, which I prefer through him. I deserve something at your Majesty's hands, for some services performed, and in consideration of the great desire I have to die in your Majesty's service; for I consider such a death the surest means of saving my soul, and the principal thing which every knight ought to desire. If God grants me children, this will be the first article of faith which I shall teach them. What I desire of your Majesty is, that, seeing that I have a hundred soldiers here, the remnant of five hundred picked men who came with me from Majorca, you will reward them according to their merits ; for in truth, Sire, they have fought well in your service, while in danger of pestilence and of the Moors. May God preserve your life for many years is the desire of your Majesty's faithful servant and vassal,

"ALONZO ENRIQUEZ DE GUZMAN."

After two months the said Francisco de Villalobos returned with the following letter from the Emperor :

"THE KING.

"Don Alonzo Enriquez de Guzman, our Captain-general of our city and island of Iviça; your servant, Francisco de Villalobos, returns with our orders, directing you to repair to our court, there to be charged with more important duties, as your service deserves. Now that the presence of the soldiers is no longer required in Iviça, you will pay them, and send them back ; and as regards the government of the city and island of Iviça, you will deliver the wand of office to Mosen Salvan. I, the King."

I attended to these instructions, first, in order to obey the commands of the Emperor, and secondly, because he promised me more important duties, in consideration of my services. I did not land the soldiers at Molverde,[1] four leagues from Valencia, where we had embarked for Majorca, but at Alicante, whence every man went to his own home.

I had almost forgotten to mention the challenge which I sent to Barbaroja, who is a tyrant. He was a man of low origin, and originally sailed from Turkey, his native country, in a small brigantine with eighteen men, and little by little, God permitting it, he rose to be King of Algiers, over fifty thousand men, whom he governs and commands. Being tired of the usual pleasures in the city of Iviça, I thought I would occupy my time by sending a challenge to this Barbaroja, which, with his reply, was as follows :

" I went to this island, where I received the news that there was a great mortality ; and, after I arrived, you sent galleys to attack us. You now have to avenge your losses, for I captured one of your vessels ; and I therefore send you this my letter of defiance, signed with my name, that you may accept it, as is the custom with Christian knights, of whom I am one. I am he who took your galley, for I came in the galleys of Majorca, with their Captain, Don Juan de Velasco, who caught the pestilence here and died. If then you desire to avenge your loss, here am I, on whom you may prove your valour, for I am he who captured your vessel ; I am he who holds your Turks in captivity ; I am he who desires to let you know who you are ; but I find nothing so bad with which to compare you, as yourself. Give an order that, as I well know that you will not come here, a fight shall take place between us, in your own country ; and if you desire company, take five of your Turks, and I will take five of my Christians. I am Don Alonzo Enriquez, of Seville, a Captain in the service of my lord the

[1] Murviedro.

Emperor and King, and I am now charged to defend the island of Iviça from your attacks. It will be necessary, if you should feel an appetite for my challenge, that you should send me security for the safety of this island, during my absence. Dated the last day of May, 1523. Those who will accompany me are Thomas de Morata, my ensign ; Juan Rodriquez, my serjeant ; Captain Perez ; Juan de Losina ; and Diego Derrano. I now conclude and seal this challenge with the seal of my arms, and my true name is

"Don Alonzo Enriquez."

"Reply of Barbaroja.

" I, Barbaroja, by the grace of God, and through my own merits and deeds of arms, King of Algiers and Captain-general, say to you, Alonzo, Captain of Iviça, that I have received your letter, and ordered it to be answered in this manner. When you are a King, as I am, you will then be in a position to send me a challenge, and I shall then be obliged to accept it. As to what you say, that I intend to attack your island of Iviça with a large force, you seem to know my intentions better than I know them myself. Written by my order."[1]

---

[1] The rise of this Barbaroja, King of Algiers, who caused so much anxiety to the Government of Charles V, was very remarkable. Two brothers, sons of a potter in the island of Lesbos, went to sea and joined a gang of pirates. The elder, called Barba-roja, from his red beard, soon became the leader of twelve piratical galleys, and spread terror through every part of the Mediterranean. At last the King of Algiers asked the pirate to assist him in an attack on the Spaniards; and Barbaroja murdered the King, and proclaimed himself King of Algiers in his room, in the year 1516. He devastated the coasts of Spain and Italy, until at last Charles V sent a force against him, and he was killed in battle in 1518. His brother, also known as Barba-roja, the same whom Don Alonzo challenged, succeeded him. This second Barba-roja, combining prudence with vigour, firmly established himself on the throne of Algiers, and extended his conquests along the coasts of Africa, placing his dominions under the protection of the Sultan, and receiving the command of the Turkish fleet. He at last, after having conquered Tunis, became so formidable, that the Emperor Charles V, as is well known, undertook an expedition against him in person, in 1535.

This reply came in Moorish, and I ordered it to be translated, as above.

XVII.

HOW I DEPARTED FROM THE PORT IN WHICH I DISEMBARKED THE
SOLDIERS.

As soon as I landed I sent a letter to the Emperor,
by a messenger, to which he replied, and the answer
reached me at Seville, for the messenger had orders to take
it to that city, where, as I believe I have already said, I
have my home. I arrived at Seville and was very well
received, with much good will, but not with any great show
of wealth, for the estates of my relations are not very equal
in amount. Some of them are very wealthy and powerful,
others are very poor, and the former did not wish to know
me, while I did not desire to know the latter. I brought
2,700 ducats with me, but I did not make this known ; and
soon the reply arrived from the Emperor, saying that I
was to repose for a few days in my own house, and, when
I was rested, to come to the court at Burgos. I then wrote
another letter to the Emperor, because I knew that he
had given away, in a Chapter lately held, a great number
of habits of the order of Santiago, of which none had fallen
to my share, although I had been promised one, and I had
since done good service. The letter was as follows :—

" My very puissant Lord,
          " I have learnt that I was left out by your Majesty,
when your Majesty distributed the habits of the order of
Santiago ; and I consider that, having defended the cities
of your Majesty against the Moors and Frenchmen, and
taken others from traitors, as is notorious, and as the royal
letters of your Majesty acknowledge, which are now in my

possession, besides other great services which, to avoid prolixity, I shall not enumerate; your Majesty should have deprived others in order to fulfil your promise to me, and not deprive me to give to others. I beseech your Majesty to reflect on the dishonour and injury which is done me, after having served so well against those who desired to do you dis-service. I beseech your Majesty then, to give me this habit of Santiago, and not to wait, as your Secretary Cobos declares is your intention, until the meeting of another Chapter, for when that will be God only knows."

To this letter the Secretary Cobos replied, that his Majesty had received it, and that he would not reply to it because every day he expected my appearance at court. I set out after a short time, as you will presently see, and in the meanwhile I remained in the city of Seville, my native place. I will now relate what happened to me there.

## XVIII.

### WHAT HAPPENED TO ME IN SEVILLE.

I have already alluded to a certain affair which happened in Flanders, relating to a challenge sent by me to Don Francisco de Mendoza, for which I was banished from the realms of Castile, owing to the great rage which the business excited in the Emperor's mind. On account of this affair I had given security to several knights in my native place, among whom was Don Pedro Enriquez de Ribera, heir of the great family and Marquisate of Tarifa. This gentleman was my great friend, but no relation, he being of the family of Enriquez of Castile, and I being of the Enriquez of Portugal. He and I proclaimed a joust, challenging all men who felt inclined to venture against us. We posted the challenge with the usual solemnity. A very important and honourable knight, of known and gentle lineage, a Regidor of the city, and Commander of the order of Santiago, treated our challenge with disdain, influenced by an old grudge. When Don Pedro Enriquez and I rode forth to an open space beyond the city, near the " Puerto del Sol," we found many knights assembled, and among them was the above-mentioned gentleman, nick-named the Commander Garçitello, who had high words with Don Juan de Guzman, my brother. The Commander had the advantage, because he came prepared with words, but they did not come to blows, owing to the presence of Francisco de Sotomayor, Count of Benalcazar, and after-wards Marquis of Ayamonte, and Duke of Bejar.[1] We afterwards went to sup in the house of my friend Don Pedro, for, both before and after he came into his inhe-ritance, he was a great lord, and what he wanted in riches, he made up in valour. When my brother, Don Juan, had related all that had passed between himself and the Commander Tello, having finished supper, Don Pedro said to me—" What do you intend to do in this matter ?" I answered that the Marquis of Ayamonte had done ill, and that one of us should go to the Commander Tello, on the part of my brother Don Juan, to ascertain his inten-tions. My friend Don Pedro agreed to this, and a follower of his was sent, named Pero Bravo, an honourable old man. He took the message to the Commander Tello, passing through the the " Calle de las armas," and, having de-livered it, the Commander answered that the Marquis heard what passed, and that he did not desire to have any words either with Don Juan, or with his brother Don Alonzo.

---

[1] He married Teresa de Zuñiga, daughter and heir of the Marquis of Ayamonte. His ancestor had been created Count of Benalcazar by Henry IV in 1466. The son, by this marriage, became Duke of Bejar, and Marquis of Ayamonte, etc.

When I knew the result, and that I was bound to be offended at the little respect shown to my brother, and the greater affront put upon myself; I used as much dissimulation as possible with Don Pedro on taking leave, saying, "I kiss your hand, my dear sir, and desire to go to bed." He replied, "Go, in God's name." Don Juan and I then went to my house, and very secretly called up the three sons of the Lord of Algaba, Don Pedro, Don Luis, and Don Rodrigo de Guzman (of whom I have given a long account already),"[1] and my brother Don Garcia, and the two brothers of my wife, Juan de Añasco and Pedro de Añasco. Altogether we numbered eight, all well armed. The Commander Tello was supping with the Marquis of Ayamonte, and we went forth to kill him, so as to pay off the new and the old grudge together, and thus confound his vanity, which was in truth extreme and unendurable, for, though his merit was great, as I have said, it was not so great as he thought, and as he desired us to think. We set out at eleven o'clock in the night, in fighting order, but very secretly, and were joined by three others, named Don Pedro de Ribera, Arnao de Zara, and Hernando de Ayala, and also by Don Pedro Enriquez. As I was walking in front I was the first to meet them, and I said to Don Pedro, "Sir, your worship does me an injury by coming out, because I rather desire that you should defend me from justice to-morrow, with your valour and power, than that you should join us against the Commander Tello to-night, for we have enough in our party for that purpose." He replied that the whole town knew that we were friends; and, as I could not persuade him to return, we all twelve went on together to the place where the Commander had gone to sup with the Marquis of Ayamonte, called the "Plaza de San Juan." Here we waited for the Commander, and presently he came, accom-

[1] See pages 18 and 19.

panied by a knight named Diego Lopez de las Roelas, another named Sandoval, his first cousin, and four men with lances. Don Juan and I came forward to Diego Lopez, while the rest of our party remained concealed behind some arcades. Before we could draw our swords, he had drawn his, but our reserve soon came up, and the said Diego Lopez, seeing that words would profit more than his sword against such odds, said, " Hold, sirs, and let not so many kill a single knight;" so we spared him. The said Commander Tello, in running away, fell down, and after he had fallen we gave him many sword cuts and stabs, and then fled to the Monastery of San Agustin, outside the walls, where we remained a month.

All this time the Commander Tello was recovering from his wounds; and afterwards the Duke of Arcos arrived from his lands, and the Licentiate Giron, who was a Judge of the Royal Chancellery, from Granada, and we were reconciled, though only in outward appearance. During all this business Don Pedro Enriquez was our friend, maintaining us with an excellent table both for ourselves and those who came to visit us, and paying all our pains and penalties, which amounted to more than two thousand ducats.

On the morning after the Commander Tello was wounded, the Marquis of Ayamonte took his wife, whose name was Dona Teresa de Zuñiga y Guzman, on the crupper of a mule, and went to see the wounded man, who was in his mother's house, as he was unmarried. On entering, the Marquis of Ayamonte said that the men who came out to stab him were twelve, while he was alone, and many other civil speeches; but he took no notice of us, at which we began to despond, especially myself, who had been the leader of the whole affair.

At the end of twelve or fourteen days, when the doctors began to entertain hopes of the Commander's life, the Marquis requested him to intercede for us, and especially for

H

Don Pedro Enriquez, who was his relation. The Commander answered that he had no intention of doing so. The Marquis then, seeing that the Commander was out of danger, set out for Ayamonte ; and finally the Commander was induced to make friends with us, through the intercession of the Duke of Arcos, whose sister was married to Don Pedro Enriquez. Thus there was an end of this affair.

## XIX.

### HOW, AFTER I WENT TO THE COURT, I FOUND THE MARQUIS OF AYAMONTE, AND ALL THE GRANDEES OF THE KINGDOM, WHO HAD BEEN SUMMONED BY THE EMPEROR TO VALLADOLID : AND WHAT HAPPENED AFTERWARDS.

I arrived in the town of Valladolid, and often visited the Duke of Bejar, to whom the Marquis of Ayamonte was heir, being married to the daughter of his brother, and the Duke not having any children, nor any nearer relations.[1] The Duke was not on good terms with the Marquis, and, when he met him by chance, either in the street or in the palace, he neither accosted him by word nor by touching his cap.

One day, when I was dining with the Duke of Bejar, he said to me : " Don Alonzo, have you heard that the Marquis of Ayamonte has bought a white horse from Don Francisco, a son of the Count of Miranda, for five hundred ducats ?" He said this in a tone of astonishment, and he had reason; for at that time the highest price for the best horse was two hundred ducats, and if three hundred ducats was given it was a fancy price. But, in truth, the excellence of the horse was not the only reason of the Marquis

---

[1] This was Don Alvaro de Zuñiga, third Duke of Bejar. He married his aunt and had no children, being succeeded by his niece, who had married the Marquis of Ayamonte.

for giving this excessive price, he also desired to please the
said Don Francisco, because he belonged to the family of
Zuñiga, to which the Dukedom appertained that he expected to inherit; and he always laboured to please the
Duke himself, as head of the family, as well as all his relations and friends.

In answering what the Duke had said, I replied that there
was no fear of his having given the five hundred ducats for
the horse, but rather for the good will of the Duke's
relations.

Before I tell you what the Duke replied to this, I desire
that you should understand that I always spoke well of
those to whom I wished well, and evil of those I wished evil;
because it appeared to me to be a vile thing to speak either
well of every body, or ill of every body. Although vengeance is prohibited in our Holy Catholic Faith, yet, as I
am not a saint, but a sinner, I trust more in the mercy of
God than in the merits of my own acts, and I retain the
consolation of hope; though it certainly is better to be a
saint than a sinner.

The Duke, on hearing my words, swore by God, and by
the body of God, that he should pay more than he thought
for in seeking for the favour of Don Francisco. On another
day, when the Marquis de los Velez and I were walking in
the colonade in front of the place, we met the Marquis of
Ayamonte, with the Count of Niebla. The Marquis said to
the Count,—" Sir, let us exchange companions, for I wish
to speak to Don Alonzo," and he took me outside the town.
When we came to the gates, he told his servants to wait, and
we went on alone. He then said, " Don Alonzo, I have
brought you here that you may hear what I have to say to
you. If you are enraged against me, it is without reason,
for if I favoured the Commander Tello against you, it was
because he had been entertained in my house, and you had
not; and in doing this I fell out with Don Pedro Enriquez

who is my first cousin, and with the others who were engaged
in the stabbing business. I have since observed that you
do not speak good of me, but evil, to the Duke, my Lord,
and I therefore would have you to understand, and I promise you on the word of a knight, that if you speak evil of
me again to the Duke, I will kill you." I replied in these
words,—" Sir, I have heard all that your Lordship has said
to me, and, answering the whole discourse briefly, I have
to say that I desire more to live in the enjoyment of your
friendship, and to be your servant, than to die in the manner
you describe, and I wish to be reconciled with you." Afterwards I sent presents to him, and so this affair came to
an end.

## XX.

### HOW I WAS PRESENTED TO THE EMPEROR, AND WHAT HAPPENED RESPECTING THE RECENT AFFAIR AT SEVILLE.

In kissing the hand of the Emperor, on arriving from
Seville, a Fleming named Falconet, to whom the Emperor
had granted the " encomienda " in Seville, which was held
by the Commander Tello, because he took it for certain that
he had died of his wounds, said to me, " How is it that you
did not kill that Commander, Don Alonzo, when your party
numbered twelve well-armed men, to kill one?" I replied
that it was true that I set out with twelve well-armed men,
because I wished to make certain of killing him, and that if
I had wanted him to kill me I should have gone alone and
unarmed. Thus I made an end of this discourse. I will
now proceed to relate what happened between his Majesty
and me, when I came to report to him the reduction of the
island of Majorca, and the defence of Iviça. I have already
told you that, when I went to the city of Seville, there hap-

pened those disputes and stabbings during the time that I was resting, according to the Emperor's orders. After the Commander Tello recovered from his wounds, I, having spoken certain words against him, he joined with his relations and spoke other offensive words of me, which caused me to challenge him to meet me alone, saying, that he should name the place, and I would go there with a sword and cloak. He went outside the city, and I went to meet him, but our relations knew of it, seized us, and made us friends, and afterwards, though we did not speak to each other, we did not bear ill will, nor do ill deeds. I now declare that the affront does not remain with me, and whosoever asserts that it does, is a liar.

## XXI.

WHAT PASSED WITH THE EMPEROR, OUR LORD, WHEN I WENT TO GIVE
AN ACCOUNT OF THE CHARGE WHICH HE HAD ENTRUSTED TO ME,
IN THE REDUCTION OF MAJORCA, AND DEFENCE OF IVIÇA.

I arrived at the Court of the Emperor, not so prosperous as the fortunate Columbus, nor so forlorn as Don Pedro de Bazan, and went at once to the house of the Secretary Cobos. I found him in bed, and he saw me as soon as I saw him, his eye was fixed on mine, and mine on his; but he was annoyed at seeing me, and did not speak for some time, because it had been reported that, in discharging what was due in my service to God and the King, I had committed acts of injustice and violence, hanging men, seducing maidens, ill-treating and defaming matrons, and permitting the robberies of my soldiers. When he spoke, he said to me that he did not desire to blame me unheard, but that I must give an account of myself to the Emperor, for that it was reported that my offences were numerous. " I counsel

you," he added, " to absent yourself, that your affairs may
be forgotten, for, I assure you, that the Emperor is now enraged against you." I replied that I was ready to answer
for all my acts, for that I was very honourable, of high birth,
and very loyal in the King's service. I also begged that a
knight, and not a lawyer, might be appointed to take my
*residencia*, for that I was sent there as a Captain and not as
a Governor, and that I did justice according to common
sense, and not according to law.

Presently he took me, on the crupper of his mule, to the
house of the Duke of Alva, Don Fadrique de Toledo,[1] who
was equally annoyed at my appearance ; but when I had
made the same explanation to him as I had done to the
Secretary Cobos, he was satisfied, and it was agreed that, on
another day, the Duke should take me to kiss the hands of
the Emperor. Accordingly we found him near the window
of an inner room, and the Duke said : " I present to your
Majesty the Viceroy of Iviça." The Emperor turned, but
said nothing, and gave me his hand unwillingly. He then
went into another room, and I returned with the Duke to
his house. On the following day, the Secretary Cobos told
me that his Majesty had ordered that my *residencia* should
be taken by Hernando de Vega, and Doctor Carbajal, a
lawyer of the Emperor's Privy Council.[2] They asked me
if it was true that I had ordered a man to be hanged because
he had no shoes ? I replied that the Moors landed and

---

[1] Don Fadrique de Toledo, the second Duke of Alva, was a cousin of
the Emperor Charles V, his mother being a sister of the Queen of Aragon, the mother of Ferdinand the Catholic. He served in Flanders, and
through all the troubles of the Comunidades.

[2] The custom in Spain, and her dependencies, was that, when any
official resigned or was recalled from his appointment, judges should be
appointed by the Government, to examine into his conduct, and hear
witnesses in evidence. This scrutiny was called a *residencia*. A very
good account of the merits and demerits of this institution is given by
Mr. Helps, *Spanish Conquest in America*, iii, p. 148-57.

surrounded a church, two leagues from the city where I and
my troops were quartered, and thus I related all the circumstances.

---

## XXII.

### HOW I FARED WITH THE RESIDENCIA, AND HOW I BECAME A COURTIER, AND WENT TO PORTUGAL.

Hernando de Vega and Doctor Carbajal were satisfied
with my account of the hanging of a soldier for not having
shoes, and soon saw that not only was it right that I should
receive no blame nor punishment, but that I deserved thanks
and rewards. Soon afterwards I went to present myself
before the Emperor, who called to me and said: " Don
Alonzo, I am well satisfied with the account you have given
of your conduct, and I consider that I have been well
served by you." After nine days, the Secretary Cobos told
me that the Emperor had appointed me to be one of the
gentlemen of his palace, and that he would give me the
habit of the order of Santiago as soon as he held another
chapter.

I then began to put my affairs in order, both as re-
garded my lodging, my person, my servants, and my horses,
effecting this with the aid of my pay, amounting to five
hundred ducats, and with the two thousand ducats which I
brought from Iviça. I remained at Court, with as much
honour to myself as possible, for three years, and during
this time the King of France was taken prisoner in a battle
in Italy.[1] When the news arrived, his Majesty was in the
town of Madrid, and he at once transmitted the tidings to
the kings who were his friends, to the nobility of his realm,
and to his cities; and, having heard from the Secretary
Cobos that half my family resided in Portugal,[2] he sent me,

[1] At the battle of Pavia, on February 24th, 1525.
[2] Don Alonzo Enriquez de Castilla, natural son of Henry II of Castille,

as one of the gentlemen of his chamber, to that country, with a letter informing the King and Queen of the capture of the said King of France. As the letter was sent open, and they did not order me to keep the contents a secret, I insert them here, as follows :

"Most serene and most excellent King, my brother. Know that the King of France was with his army in Italy, near the city of Pavia, and my Captain-General gave him battle, and took prisoner the said King, and routed his army, as Don Alonzo Enriquez de Guzman, a gentleman of my royal house, will more fully inform you, having received the news from a gentleman who brought it to me, and whom I do not send, because he was very tired. May God preserve your most serene and most excellent royal person. From Madrid.                 " THE KING.

                                   " COBOS, Secretary."

I also brought another letter for the Queen his wife, sister of the Emperor, and when I arrived, I dismounted at the house of the Ambassador, who notified my arrival to the King and Queen. The King sent to say that he would see me the next day, Saturday, and it was not known how he would receive the news; for though the Emperor was his brother-in-law and friend, yet the King of France was a Christian, and was not his enemy. On Saturday he sent to

was created by that King, Count of Gijon and Noroña, in 1373. Our author, Don Alonzo, was descended from a natural son of this Count, his ancestors having settled in Seville. This Count of Gijon married Isabella, a daughter of Ferdinand King of Portugal, and his legitimate children settled in that country. One of his sons was Archbishop of Lisbon, and his daughter, Constance, married Alonzo, first Duke of Braganza, but had no issue. The descendants of his sons, with the name of Noroña, were nearly all established in Portugal.

The family of Enriquez, Admirals of Castille, is quite distinct from the families of Enriquez of Seville, and of Portugal. The Admirals of Castille of this family were descended from Don Alonzo Enriquez, son of Don Fadrique de Castilla, who was grandson of King Alonzo XI of Castille.

put off the interview until Sunday after dinner, and accordingly, at that hour, I went with the Ambassador, who was
named Juan de Zuñiga.  I was also accompanied by the
Count of Villanova, who married my cousin, the Captain-
General of the island of Madeira, the Count of " las Desi-
ertas,"[1] married to a sister of my father, and Don Juan de
Guzman, and Don Garcia de Guzman, my brothers,[2] who
were here at the time, though natives of Seville.

We found the King[3] in a room, surrounded by bishops,
lords, and other people; and I went on my knees on the
ground, kissed the letter of the Emperor, presented it, and
rose again.  He began to read the letter, and, when he had
finished, he said to me: " Don Alonzo Enriquez de Guzman,
the Emperor writes that you can inform me how the King
of France was taken prisoner.  I, therefore, beseech you to
do so, if it is not troublesome to you."  All this time he was
sitting in a chair, and I was standing somewhat lower down.
I then went on my knees, kissed his hand, rose again, and
spoke as follows.  " The army of the King of France being
encamped near the city of Pavia in Lombardy, the King
being with it in person, and desiring to usurp the jurisdiction of the said city by force, together with the kingdom,
he performed many violent and unjust acts, bringing the
name of Christianity into discredit.  One night the Marquis
of Pescara, with two thousand musketeers, forced an entrance over the entrenchments of the French, and in the
battle the King of France, with many other knights, was
taken prisoner.  His army was so utterly routed that not a
man remained; all were either taken, killed, wounded, or
put to flight."  The King replied thus : " Don Alonzo En-

---

[1] This was Juan Gonzalez de Camara de Lobos, married to our author's
aunt, Doña Maria de Noroña.  He was second in command in the island
of Madeira.

[2] These were his half brothers, who settled in Madeira.

[3] This was King John III of Portugal, son of King Manuel.

I

riquez, inform the Emperor that I am much pleased at any good fortune which may befall him, especially this, which will lead to universal peace in Christendom."

I then retired, perceiving that the interview was at an end, and I went to the lodging of the Queen his wife, who was sitting in a corridor. I gave her the letter, and, when she had read it, she said: "Don Alonzo Enriquez, I understand that you have not yet dined, and I shall expect a long account of all that has happened from you; therefore I desire that you will first refresh yourself." So I went, with my companions, to dine, and the Queen did not send for me again until an hour before dusk. The King was with her, and we three remained talking until an hour after dark, when the King rose, took the Queen by the hand, and we went into a corridor, where we found the Infanta, his sister, with all the ladies of the Court, and the Infantes his brothers, Don Luis and Don Fernando. There were musicians and singers, and, after we were seated, the music began, and knights and ladies danced both after the Christian and the Moorish fashion. At this time a lady of the Infanta's court, named Dona Leonora de Castro, having obtained permission from the lady with whom I was sitting, who was a niece of my own, sat down beside me and told me that she was enamoured of me, and that she was resolved to do me a service. I presently saw what she desired, and determined to give her my hands, and something more if she wished it, although she was ugly. She then said: "Do not make yourself so great a lord with me, but become my equal," and I replied that all the advantages I had over her should count as nothing, and that I would become her equal, but that it was necessary that she should give her consent. We were occupied in this foolish talk during the whole evening, and, when we parted, she begged, as it was not proper that she should seek me, that I would come to dine with the Infanta, her mistress.

## XXIII.

### HOW I DINED WITH THE INFANTA OF PORTUGAL.

On the following day I entered the room where the Infanta was dining, when she had nearly finished, and the Emperor's Ambassador came with me. Our entrance caused much confusion and disturbance, both in the serenity of the most serene Infanta, and in the minds of the attendant ladies. As these ladies had not yet risen from the table, I went straight to my damsel of the previous night, who received me with great delight. You may well believe that our intercourse was very discreet and secret, because, after her mistress was married to the Emperor, she married the eldest son of the Duke of Gandia. While we were talking much in the same way as we did on the previous evening, they rose from the table, and I approached the Infanta and said : " Madam, the Emperor, my Lord, has sent me to the most serene and most excellent King and Queen, with news of the capture of the King of France, and the defeat of his army, and I did not wish to return without speaking to you, and kissing your royal hands. I beseech you, therefore, to pardon my audacity." She replied : " Don Alonzo Enriquez de Guzman, I congratulate you on the news which you have brought, and I remember well that you are half a Portuguese ;" she then laughed, and I also laughed, and became more enamoured of the Infanta than of her damsel. I was five days in Portugal, and on each day a thousand affairs of this kind occurred. When I was about to depart, the King and Queen gave me letters for the Emperor, with thirty cruzados, of ten ducats each, from the King, and twenty from the Queen, making in all five hundred ducats in our Castillian money. I took them, though I certainly regretted that they gave me no more, and so I departed to return to the Emperor's court.

## XXIV.

### WHAT AFTERWARDS BEFELL ME WITH THE EMPEROR.

Returning by the post, as I had come, I met the Duke of
Alva in a litter, and alighted to kiss his hand; but he would
not let me speak until I had come up into the litter with
him.   He then showed me a letter which the Emperor had
written, saying that he was about to leave the town of
Madrid, and to go to Nuestra Señora de Guadaloupe.   The
Duke desired that I should not go on by post, but remain
with him, and, as a Duke's desire is a command, I wrote to
the Secretary Cobos to explain the reason of my delay, and
continued with the Duke.   The Duke and I passed our time
in a way that made me afterwards feel that those lines were
perfectly true—

> " The moments that are speeding fast
>   We heed not, but the past,—the past,—
>   More highly prize ;"[1]

for, within the litter, we made merry, and laughed, and
joked.

When the Duke and I arrived at Guadaloupe, we were
well received by the Friars, and after five days the Emperor
came.   I went to kiss his hand on the day after his arrival,
and to give an account of my mission, the Duke accompanying me.   Having made my report, he said : " Don Alonzo,
you have performed this service well, and now tell me freely
about the people you saw in Portugal."   I said : " Sire, I
saw a King who was fat, short, with a scanty beard, and not
very discreet.   I saw his Queen, who was stately to behold,

---

[1] Here Don Alonzo quotes the famous poem of Don Jorge Manrique,
the son of the Count of Paredes, who was killed at Cañavete in 1479,
which has been so well translated by Longfellow :
> " Quan presto se va el placer
>   Como despues de acordado
>   Da dolor."

very honourable and wise, and with her I saw an Infanta, who was all that could be desired." He then asked me if the Infante Don Luis was as tall as himself, and many other questions, and as soon as I had satisfied him, he said that he wished to hear more of the Infanta, and I told him many things respecting her beauty, her learning, her modesty, and her youth. It was not only on this day that he asked me about her, but he continued to do so on other occasions.

## XXV.

THE HOSTILITY OF THE BISHOP OF OSMA, THE KING'S CONFESSOR, AGAINST
ME ; AND THE FRIENDSHIP OF MY LADY DONA MARIA DE MENDOZA,
WIFE OF THE SECRETARY COBOS, GRAND COMMANDER OF THE ORDER
OF SANTIAGO ; AND OF THE KINDNESS SHE SHEWED ME, KNOWING
THAT HER HUSBAND WAS MY FRIEND ; AND OF OTHER EVENTS
DOWN TO THE TIME WHEN THE EMPEROR MARRIED.

The Bishop of Osma was a friar of the order of Santo Domingo, and so sharp, diligent, and cunning, that they made him General of the order, and afterwards his reputation rose so high that he became Confessor to the Emperor, and Bishop of Osma. Dona Maria de Mendoza, the wife of the Secretary Cobos, Grand Commander of the order of Santiago, was the eldest daughter of Don Juan Hurtado de Mendoza, Count of Ribadavia, by Maria Sarmiento, his wife. This Dona Maria, in addition to being daughter of such a father and such a mother, who were of very noble lineage, was herself most gracious and honourable, respected by all the world, offending no one, doing good to many and evil to none. She was most Christian, affable, and entertaining, very gentle and charitable, and most beautiful.[1]

[1] This lady was a daughter of Don Juan Hurtado de Mendoza and his wife, Maria Sarmiento, daughter and heir of the Count of Ribadabia.

I was admitted to the friendship of this lady as well as to
that of her husband; but she, being a woman, felt more
for my misfortunes, and supplied me with breakfasts, and
clothes, and presents, as if I had been her own brother.

One day this lady and I, and her brothers, and two other
ladies, named Isabel de Quintanilla and Catalina de Laso,
were resting ourselves in a garden, the court being then at
Madrid, and, after having eaten a collation, we ran about
after each other until one of the party fell down so heavily
as to be stunned and appear dead. My lady Dona Maria,
and the other ladies, believing that he was so, wept and
bemoaned piteously. Presently the Archbishop of Toledo
came to see the garden, and with him the said Bishop Confessor, and Dona Maria accosted them, briefly stating what
had happened. The Confessor replied as if he thought the
man was dead, and blamed the lady, which caused me to
look upon him as my enemy. This occurred before I went
to Portugal, and the Queen, when I started on my return,
not being aware of our enmity, gave me a letter to the said
Bishop Confessor, which she charged me to deliver into his
hands. I met him in the cloister of the monastery of Gauda-
loupe, which adjoined the apartments of the Emperor, and
he thought I was going to ask him for absolution, because
it was Lent; and he said that at this season our Lady
worked miracles. I gave him the letter, and, when he had
read it, he said: " The Queen of Portugal has many times
desired me to propose the marriage of the Emperor with
the lady Infanta, her sister-in-law, and it is certainly my
duty to obey her orders, as the sister of the Emperor, and
on account of the merits of the Infanta herself. It is my
desire that the Emperor should marry her Highness, for the
Infanta of England, concerning whom there have been nego-

The lady Maria de los Cobos, in her turn became heiress of Ribadabia,
and her son, by the Secretary Don Francisco de los Cobos, was Count
of Ribadabia.

ciations, is a child, and also more foreign to our manners and feelings." As soon as I saw that he had finished his discourse, the whole of which I have not given here, because it would fill another book larger than this, I said : " Sir, the enmity which I felt against you is now at an end, and I am ready to assist you in this affair of the Infanta." He answered : " Well, Don Alonzo, we now understand each other respecting this marriage ; the labour shall be shared between us, but the reward shall be all yours. This afternoon we shall be with the Emperor, and if he should speak to you concerning the affairs of Portugal, you must talk of the Infanta, and I will take occasion to mention the letter which the Queen wrote to me ; for the marriage with the Infanta of England is almost arranged, and the Emperor shows so much modesty in talking of his marriage, and the succession to the kingdom, as to say that his heirs are the King of Hungary and his sons ; and he shows this not only by words, but by the colour of his face."

We then parted, not without many ceremonies and expressions of friendship, and in the afternoon we met in the presence of the Emperor, who asked me whether I wished to talk in Portuguese or in Spanish. I replied that any language would be honoured by being used, in speaking of the beauty, the modesty, and the excellence of the Infanta of Portugal. I then left him conversing with the Bishop of Osma, and on the following day the said Bishop invited me to dinner, and told me all that had passed. " I would have you to know," he said, " that the Emperor is very modest and chaste ; but I induced him to converse on the subject of his marriage."

## XXVI.

### HOW THE EMPEROR WAS MARRIED, AND THE REWARD WHICH HIS WIFE GAVE ME.

The Emperor determined to marry the said lady Infanta of Portugal, and if you will not believe that I assisted, at least believe that I did not hinder the affair, and if my labour was without authority, it was done for love and good-will. When the Emperor went to Seville, which is my native country, to be married, he was accompanied by the Marquis of Villareal, the chief nobleman in Portugal, who is my cousin.[1] We went together to Her Majesty, and the Marquis said to her, " Madam, I bring with me Don Alonzo Enriquez, who deserves much, both on account of his lineage and his deeds. He is my relation, and you owe much to his good offices in the affair of your marriage." I then said, " The Marquis has done me a favour in thus speaking of me to your Majesty, and I would add that my service consisted in always speaking well of you, to his Majesty and to all men." Her Majesty answered not a word, which we attributed to her modesty, having been but recently married. I waited for some days, and then I besought her to obtain for me the habit of the order of Santiago from the Emperor. She said she would do so, but her delays were so long, that at last I went to my former love, Dona Leonora de Castro, and said, " Lady, thine eyes have conquered me, and may it please God that I may be as fortunate a lover in Castile, as I was in Portugal." As I have before said, this lady was very discreet, and she replied that she knew my deserts, and that if she was the Empress I should have them :

---

[1] Charles V set out for Seville to be married in 1526, after having set his prisoner Francis at liberty, and seen him some leagues on his way to France. The wedding was celebrated with extraordinary magnificence in Seville, but the festivities were interrupted by the death of the Emperor's sister Isabel, Queen of Denmark.

she also promised to speak to her mistress, and I told her
that I had long tried to obtain the habit of the order of
Santiago from the Emperor, but that I had never been able
to succeed.

## XXVII.

### HOW I RECEIVE A PENSION.

Two or three months after his marriage, the Emperor
went from Seville to the city of Granada, towards the end
of summer.  I now found myself in debt, and ill paid,
while the Emperor was occupied with his recent marriage
which I had negotiated.  At last, after many representations, I said to him, " Sire, it is now four years since I
entered your household, after having defended your towns
from the Moors and Frenchmen, and as a reward you gave
me ninety thousand maravedis a year, with the title of a
gentleman of your house, and five hundred ducats in money,
with the hope of the habit of the order of Santiago.  I am
married, and yet have I been ten years of my life in your
service, and absent from my wife, and the four last years I
have passed in the hope of obtaining the order, for which I
had formerly importuned your Majesty." In consequence
of this appeal the Emperor ordered a pension to be given
me ; and he issued an edict, as follows : " These are to let
our chief accountants know, that, for many loyal and distinguished services which Don Alonzo Enriquez de Guzman,
a gentleman of our house, has performed, both in the capture of Captain Martin, our traitor, on the sea ; in the
attack on Los Gelves in Barbary, and on Tournay in France ;
in the surrender of Majorca, and in the defence of the city
and island of Iviça against the Moors and Frenchmen, we
order the sum of seventy thousand maravedis a year to be
paid to him for the remainder of his life, in three payments,

K

at the end of every four months, neither a day sooner nor a
day later. This pension is to be paid from the revenues of
Seville, and this order shall be your authority, which is to
be entered in your books, and the original returned to the
said Don Alonzo." I then retired to my home, and at the
end of a year, a little more or less, the chapter was held in
which I was promised the habit of the order of Santiago.

## XXVIII.

### HOW I FARED IN MY ATTEMPT TO OBTAIN THE HABIT OF THE ORDER OF SANTIAGO.

The Emperor, in this year, convoked a Cortes both of the
nobles of the kingdom and of the procurators of cities, and
held chapters of all the three orders, Santiago, Calatrava,
and Alcantara: for he had received news from the King of
Hungary, of the hostile designs of the Turk. They assembled in the town of Valladolid, and I also went there in
search of the habit of the order of Santiago. In truth, as I
have just been on the point of saying in several parts of this
book, when I sought for the habit, I did so on account of
the position it would give, without knowing the trouble and
difficulty the attempt would bring upon me. As the time
passed away without my being able to obtain it, those who
wished me ill insinuated false suspicions against me. When
I arrived at Valladolid, I found the Emperor with all his
nobles and procurators of cities. I came in company with
Don Pedro Enriquez de Ribera of Seville, heir of the Marquis of Tarifa, who was a man of rare qualities, a true friend,
and very frank, though not rich. There was no relationship
between us that I know of, yet he always liked my company,
and thus we came together to the town of Valladolid.

I went to speak with the Emperor, and said: "Sire, you
know well how much I desire the habit of the order of

Santiago, and you have promised to confer it on me, in the first chapter that is assembled : refresh your memory, and fulfil your promise." He replied: " Don Alonzo, they are about to chant the ' Gloria ;' " and six months passed away, at the end of which the Emperor went to Palencia, giving orders that I was not to go with him. The Prior of San Juan, who is one of the most distinguished men in the kingdom, and who, as I have before mentioned in this book, is named Don Diego de Toledo,[1] now came forward as my friend. He was a good Christian, very fond of hearing sermons and attending mass, very noble and liberal and honourable, being haughty with the proud, and humble with the lowly, willing to do good to many, and evil to no man, even if it were to his own hindrance. He asked me to come with him to visit his home, and I replied that I kissed the hands of his lordship, but that I had waited so long for the habit of the order of Santiago, that I did not now wish to be out of the way. The Prior then spoke to the Emperor, who, on the following day, said to me : " Don Alonzo, it is well that you should go with the Prior, for no one will go with me to Palencia, excepting my attendants, and I will remember you, just as if you were present." The Prior and I then went to the Secretary Cobos, and the Prior told the Secretary all that had passed, and of his intention to take me with him, begging him to look after my interests during my absence.

After two months a letter arrived from the Secretary Cobos for the Prior, and another for me. In this letter to me he said that it was not wise to importune Kings, especially in an affair on which his Majesty was so determined, as he was to withhold from me the habit, and that I must have patience. Eight days afterwards I departed, and the Prior of San Juan assisted and favoured me, both with money, and with letters to the Emperor, to his Confessor,

[1] See page 22.

and to the Secretary Cobos, urging my claims to the habit of the order of Santiago.

With these letters I went to Burgos, where the court then was, and proceeded to the lodging of the Confessor. I told him that, if I did not receive the habit, I would never return home, but would go very far away, that I might not give occasion for my enemies to rejoice, nor for my friends to mourn. The Confessor asked me to dine with him, and afterwards the Secretary Cobos entered, and they agreed together to speak to the Emperor in my favour. The Secretary asked me to supper to meet his wife, the lady Maria, who was very angry because I had not alighted at her lodging, as I had been accustomed to do. After four days the Secretary and the Confessor told me that they had spoken to the Emperor, and that the affair was progressing favourably. When I had an interview with his Majesty, he said that when I had enraged him by what I had done in Flanders, he had sworn that I should not have the habit of Santiago. I answered: " Sire, all oaths which are made in opposition to honour are not valid," and he told me to speak to Cobos, and passed into another room. Ten days afterwards the Secretary Cobos told me that the Emperor would give me the habit; but that, as there were almost as many persons who wished me ill as those who wished me well, it would be very necessary to produce proofs of my lineage.

## XXIX.

THE EMPEROR GOES TO ITALY, AND I AM BANISHED FOR TRYING TO KILL THE ACCOUNTANT.

I went with the Emperor, when he removed the court to Madrid, and on the road there was a large village with a very strong house, called Vuytrago, belonging to the Duke of Ynfantado, and the Emperor alighted at the door, while all his followers went to their lodgings, excepting myself. A man of short stature, with a black beard, and matted hair, threw himself on his knees before his Majesty, in front of the staircase, and said : " I am a servant of the Duke of Ynfantado, your vassal, and when I heard of your Majesty's journey from Burgos to Madrid, I made such preparations as I was able." We entered a large saloon adorned with tapestry of silk and gold, and embroidered with figures of the olden time, with a very large canopy. This led to another room with very rich silken tapestry, and a bed of brocade. The little black-bearded Chamberlain walked before us, and presently he conducted us to another richly hung room, with a crimson canopy enriched with gold. The Emperor sat down in a chair, and I rested myself on a stool, and afterwards he retired to an inner room, while I went to my lodging, supping in a kitchen, and undressing in a kitchen. The next morning his Majesty departed, and we arrived at Madrid.

From Madrid the Emperor went to reside at Toledo, where he resolved upon his journey to Italy; and I, being lodged in the house of the Secretary Cobos, knew of this determination before many others. One evening I found the Emperor in conversation with his courtiers, and, entering, said—" Sire, I offer my person and estate in your service, to go to Italy"; but he told me that I could serve him as well here as there, and that it was better that I should kill rabbits on my own hills, and eat them, than that the sea should kill me, and the fishes should eat me. So I kissed his hand, and returned to my own home in Seville, where I remained for seven or eight months.

I was driven from Seville, through the machinations of those who wished me ill there. The Count of Andrade was one of my enemies, and persecuted me until I went to the Empress, our lady, and to her Royal Council, and complained of his conduct. The Empress assisted me with money; but my pension was ill paid by the Accountant Sanchez, who was a fat ill-conditioned old Biscayan. In trying to recover my money, I attempted to kill the Accountant and his son, and was arrested, imprisoned in the house of an Alguazil, and afterwards banished five leagues from the court.

## XXX.

### WHAT HAPPENED TO ME IN MY BANISHMENT, WITH THE DUKE OF INFANTADO, AND WITH THE MARQUIS OF VILLENA, DUKE OF ESCALONA.

At this time the Court was at Madrid, and I thought that Santa Cruz would be a good place at which to pass my exile, being five leagues from Madrid, and two from Guadalaxara, and belonging to Don Alonzo de Azevedo, Archbishop of Toledo. I went to an inn, gave plenty of provender to my horses, and ordered my servants, for want of other meat, to kill and eat the fowls; thinking that my friend the Duke of Infantado would presently send me plenty of fowls and barley.[1] But the landlord asked me whether, if the Duke did not send, I had money to pay the bill. I said yes, and that my servants were to have a fowl for dinner and a fowl for supper each, every day, and my beasts plenty of barley. I then wrote to the Duke, and asked him to assist me; but eight days passed away, all the fowls in the place were eaten, and no reply came, although I had begged him to send me fifty ducats. I then sent another letter, but the Duke sent back to say he had a pain in his stomach, and so I and my servants supped that night on a very light salad.

Next day I paid the bill, and went to Yllescas, eight

---

[1] This was Don Diego Hurtado de Mendoza, third Duke of Infantado.

leagues from Escalona, sending a letter to the Duke[1] of the place, in which I said :—" Most Illustrious Sir, although our acquaintance has been slight, yet my desire to serve you has never been small; and I would now have you to know that I am banished from the Court, and am in great want of fifty dobloons, which I beseech you to send me." He not only sent me the money, but invited me to Escalona, where I was lodged with the Duke and his beautiful lady, and when I departed he gave me a hundred double ducats. Thence I went to Toledo, where I found my lady Maria, wife of the Secretary Cobos, visiting her father, the Count of Ribadavia, who was Corregidor of the city. He wrote to the President of the Royal Council, asking him to negotiate my pardon with the Empress; in consequence of which an order arrived, limiting the period of my banishment to six months.

---

## XXXI.

### HOW I RETURNED TO COURT.

I visited Seville, and afterwards returned to the Court, which was then at Medina del Campo, to kiss the hands of the President, who was named Don Juan Tabara. He had resided a long time in Seville, and was a great friend of my father. Afterwards he was Archbishop of Santiago and President of the Royal Council, and always stood by me as a friend. I also wished to see Dona Maria Madalena, daughter of the Count of Osorno, and my very good lady. I went to the palace, and saw the lady Dona Leonora de Castro, who had been my love, and who sent for me to kiss

---

[1] This was Don Diego Lopez de Pacheco, second Duke of Escalona and Marquis of Villena. He distinguished himself in the last Moorish war in Granada, and died in 1529. The first Duke was created in 1470.

her hands, in her own house; and introduced me to her husband, Don Francisco de Borja, eldest son of the Duke of Gandia. They invited me to dinner, and I remained there eight days without kissing the hands of the Empress; and when I went to take leave of the President, he asked if I had presented myself before Her Majesty? I said no, and he exclaimed: "Holy Mary! this is a bad business." I then went, but not from any good will, sending to say that I was in attendance. The Empress asked me why I was enraged with her? and I replied that, in spite of all that I had done after my journey to Portugal, she had not been my friend with the Emperor.

## XXXII.

### HOW ONCE MORE I DEPARTED FROM THE COURT.

At this time I was seized with a quartan fever, which lasted a long year; and hearing that the Duke of Alva had died of the same illness, I travelled towards Astorga, where his son, the Prior of St. John, my good friend, was staying. The Marquis of Miranda was there, and entertained me for ten days, and I went out hunting three times on a white horse, with brocade trappings. Thence I went to Zamora, on my way to Seville, lodging with Enrique de Guzman, son of the Count of Alba de Liste, who is married to Dona Maria de Toledo, granddaughter of the Duke of Alva, the most beautiful lady mentioned in this book, excepting Dona Maria de Mendoza. Both husband and wife treated me very kindly, as well with delicate viands, as with courteous civility. Two doctors, who were there, cured me and gave me directions how to keep off the fever. They said that melons were good both in summer and winter, and recommended capers and artichokes; as well as wild apples, boars, rabbits, and partridges.

I will also relate what a Franciscan Friar, confessor to the Prior of St. John, said to me. "Sir," he said, "I understand that you have been ill for some days, that your disease is a quartan fever, and that you are choked by phlegm. You must understand that this is a divine judgment on you, for your evil deeds. If you wish to recover, you must reform; for I know not what profit or pleasure you can find in speaking evil of your neighbours, whom Christ, our Redeemer, has desired us to love as ourselves. Not only you do not love them, but you hate, disdain, and dishonour them; and if you choose to continue doing so, you will enjoy little in this world, and will be paid in the next with endless misery." I replied—"Reverend father! when God made neighbours, he did not make them wicked; and you must not take it ill that I abuse bad men. It is not wise to speak well of every one; for if we speak not ill of some, it is of no avail to speak well of others." He then said—"But, sir, I have heard that in Seville, your native town, you speak evil of many persons without reason." I answered—"Pardon me, good father, you cannot know my reasons, at least not so well as I know them myself; for if a man is not my friend, and does not support me, even though he is not my enemy, and does not act against me, yet I will complain of him, and treat him as an enemy. God said, by the Evangelist, He who is not for me is against me; and, as sick men have liberty to dismiss visitors, pray begone, in God's name, O reverend father."

Next day I went to Salamanca and lodged at an inn; and the day after I came to Alva de Tormes, where I heard that the old duke had died like a saint, and that his grandson, Don Hernan Alvarez de Toledo, had succeeded. The new duke received me very well, lodging me in his own chamber, with our beds side by side; and on the fourth day, when my fever returned, the duchess came up to see me, as if I had

L

been her brother. After twenty days I again set out for Seville, well supplied with mules, clothes, and money.

In due time I arrived at Seville; but I must not omit to relate the death of the most valorous, Christian, and humane Prince, the Duke of Alva, Don Fadrique de Toledo, grandfather of his successor, Don Hernan Alvarez. He treated kings as lords, and they treated him as a companion and friend; he was affable and gentle to all men, alike with wise and foolish, friars and children, great and small. His death was caused by a tertian fever, having lived seventy-five years. One day before his death he sat up in his bed, and sent for the Bishop of Cordova, the Prior of San Juan, Don Diego de Toledo and his sons, and the Count of Alba de Liste, and said: " Sons, I believe that I shall die to-morrow, for I am weak and without pulse. I charge you all to persevere in honour and faithful service." They began to weep, and he to console them, saying that he was going to life eternal. He then confessed, received the holy sacrament, and yielded his soul to God. His successor joined the Emperor in Flanders, and obediently followed the commands of his grandfather.

---

## XXXIII.

THE FOLLOWING LETTER WAS ONE WHICH I WROTE TO ANOTHER KNIGHT, NAMED PERO MEXIA, BECAUSE WE HAD PROMISED EACH OTHER THAT, IF THE ALMIGHTY GOD PERMITTED IT, THE FIRST OF US THAT DIED SHOULD APPEAR TO THE OTHER.

Sir,—I do not forget that I promised to you, and that you made the same promise to me, that he who died first should appear to the other. I would now have you to know that, on leaving this city, my legs began to swell, and my teeth to ache. Thus, stumbling along in a sorry fashion, I came to Valladolid, afterwards to Madrid, and thence to Monçon in Aragon, where I experienced a hundred thousand strange and terrible feelings; and at last I fell ill of a fever. In my bed I turned my mind to spiritual things, and prepared to die in the way which is ordained by my religion. My soul was filled with anxiety, I was attacked with giddiness and vomiting, I almost lost my senses, the extremities of my feet became cold, and I knew what death was, although I did not actually experience it. Then the chill rose up from my feet as high as my knees, and presently I was seized with intolerable pain, as if the points of pins had been stuck under my nails. My legs felt as if they did not belong to me, my maladies laid siege to my life, and at last I resolved to surrender, and place myself in the hands of God. Terrible pains came upon me, as if my skin was being torn from my flesh; so I rose up and said—" Domine comendo espiritum meum." Then a great agony came upon me, with a rattle in the throat; and it seemed as if my soul had gone forth in pain, as when a woman gives birth to a child.

I thought that I saw the soul outside the body, naked and terrified in the midst of a vile crew, for sixty devils were with me. I looked at the body, and it seemed vile, worn out, and covered with blood; the eyes wide open but vacant, for they could see nothing; the mouth open, but it could not speak; the tongue hanging out, but it could not taste. Then I turned to God and said—"O Lord, thou who dwellest in Heaven, to thee I raise my eyes." When I had finished, I took the hand of the good angel whom God had appointed to watch over me, and sang the following verse— " Dilexisti justitiam et odisti iniquitatem." Then all the angels, good and bad, cried out, saying—" This soul is ours, and belongs to us." The bad angels said—" This soul was always sinful, incredulous, without faith, without charity, without mercy; it committed many great crimes on earth."

My soul then went past the palaces of rubies; and with all my tribulation I desired to have tidings of my friends, and especially to ask the deceased treasurer, Alonzo Gutierrez, whether for money one might enter the seventh Heaven. At this time my good angel answered the devils, and said that though what they had said might be true, yet that I had turned to God before my death, and that I had confessed, communicated, and yielded up the fortress of my body in the way which is prescribed by the holy Catholic Church.

St. Michael answered, "O Evil Ones, you have no share in this soul; for though it was sinful, it was not so sinful as you are. And you, O soul, because you desired evil to your enemies in Seville, I ordain that, on returning to earth, you shall not go to Seville, but that you shall live in your house at Santiponçe, feed upon roast meat, and be content."

Thus, Sir, in summer I intend to rise at five o'clock, wear shoes and doublet, and a long cloak, and feed on a roast duck, and in the winter I shall have an *olla podrida* warming under the chimney. Now I commend you to God. Dated in Monçon, where I was disembodied, on the 10th of July, 1533. Speaking seriously, and in my right mind, I swear by God and the Holy House at Jerusalem, that I desire to end my days and to die as a Christian, and your servant.

-----

## XXXIV.

THIS IS A LETTER WHICH THE BISHOP OF ESCALAS WROTE TO ME, BECAUSE I HAD WRITTEN TO ASK HIM WHETHER HE HAD SEEN THE LETTER WHICH I WROTE TO PERO MEXIA.

Sir,—I have received a letter from you, without knowing whence it came or where it was written. It had neither head nor tail, and professed to be in reply to six or seven of mine which you say you have received.   In truth, I never have written them, and the two good knights—Intention and Desire—must take the credit, for I have intended to write six or seven times.

You tell me that Pero Mexia has received a letter from you, giving an account of your death, so that I must infer that you are dead.   O cursed be that death, which has come so suddenly upon you, while it approaches others so slowly.   O unhappy Dona Constança, that you should suffer such a loss; O most unlucky Santiponçe to lose such an owner.   Requiescat in pace.   Amen.

But since you, Sir, are the body and soul of the deceased Don Alonzo, I would remind you that broilers in this world know more about cellars than about Ave Marias, and I say this as a theologian.   How shall such men, who were never at peace in this world, expect peace in the world to come?   He who always lives in the midst of broils and quarrels, seldom dies in peace.   If it be true that Don Alonzo is dead, it is a pity, for if my Lady Curse-all or my Lord Curse-all were to be lost, this Don Alonzo would be sure to find them again.   Dated in Seville; from the Bishop of Escalas, who kisses your hand.

## XXXV.

### WHAT HAPPENED TO ME, AFTER MY RETURN TO SEVILLE, AND HOW I SET OUT FOR THE INDIES.

My enemies in Seville continued to persecute me, and seeing their determination to ruin me, especially the friends of the Commander Tello, both by speaking the truth and by telling lies, and that I was poor in estate, and not rich in relations (for though I am related to the greatest families both in Portugal and Castile, yet I derive no benefit from them), I determined to seek for fortune elsewhere.   I re-

solved to proceed to one of three places, either to serve with
my lord the Emperor; or to go to Naples, where a son of
the Duke of Alva is Viceroy; or to sail for the Indies. The
latter plan was difficult to execute, because they tell me that
there are a hundred thousand wild and strange beasts which
might send me out of this present world, besides sufferings
and hardships to endure; added to which I considered, that
having once served under a King, it was not well to begin
to serve under Viceroys.

It is, however, necessary to understand that in these
Indies there is much gold and silver, as well as dangers and diseases, and that where there is much to gain
there is also much risk. I have, therefore, adopted the
motto, " He who does not fear death, enjoys life," which I
caused to be embroidered on my flags in letters of gold, in
the companies I have commanded as captain. In the year
of our Lord 1533, during Lent, I confessed and received the
most holy sacrament, as every faithful Christian ought to do.
Amongst other things which I then did, was to declare, as I
now declare, that many things in this book, both to improve
the style, and to give an appetite to him who reads it, are not
related exactly as they happened, though the substance is
true: I therefore desire that each reader may believe as
much as he ought to believe, so that neither his conscience
nor mine may be hurt.

After much reflection, considering the cruel neglect with
which the Emperor treated me, in spite of all the great services I had performed for him, in defending his towns from
Moors and Frenchmen, I at last resolved to go to the Indies,
and see the barbarous Indians. I embarked in the month of
September 1533 with two esquires, and two pages, a supply
of provisions, and all that was necessary for a long voyage.
The ship made sail on the last day of September, and we
pursued our voyage to the Indies. Having embarked all
my property, and taken leave of my friends and relations, I

determined to undertake many enterprises before my return, confiding in the just Judge, the Almighty God, and also in the most Christian Emperor Charles, our King and Lord who now reigns. We came to again off the town of San Lucar. The name of the ship was *Santa Maria la bella*, and while we waited for the time of sailing, I wrote a letter to the Emperor, as follows :

" Most powerful Lord,

" I, who now write, defended your towns from the Moors and the Frenchmen, and spent my money in your service, being a captain and gentleman of your palace ; but I have received in return malice and envy from my enemies, who have traduced me before your Royal Council. They at last obtained an order, signed by your Royal hand, in which my departure to the Indies is prohibited, as a traitor, thief, and murderer. A false account has been given to your Majesty ; but I confide in your Christian, just, and sacred judgment, and I do not obey the said order because I have not seen it ; and I trust that the only evils prepared for me are the dangers of the sea and of the Indies. May God preserve the most serene and powerful person of your Majesty many years. From the servant and humble vassal of your Majesty,

" ALONZO ENRIQUEZ DE GUZMAN."

Presently I beheld the ship, on board of which was my property and my intention, make sail, but my body remained on shore. I, however, got into a boat with five of my servants, and caught up the ship about three leagues from San Lucar. The Captain, having received the order for my detention from the Council, called out to me from the poop : " Don Alonzo, you must not come on board ;" yet, by soft and flattering words, I at last reached the deck, but the Captain and sailors, with drawn swords, stopped me and said I could not remain in the ship. My own people rallied round me, and finally the sailors yielded, and I continued my voyage. I really believe, and you may also believe, that they only intended to obey their orders, and that they did not wish to kill me, nor that I should kill them.

I must now defend myself from the blame which may be imputed to me for undertaking this adventure. It is true that I had an income by means of which I might have lived, though miserably, but I desired to have more. I left some houses in Seville, which would support my wife, who is a very dutiful and Christian woman, and I took care that her home should be well supplied with all that she required, and now that I am safe on board I may say that I have four thousand ducats with me.

Seven days after sailing from San Lucar de Barrameda we arrived at the Canary Islands, and I landed on the island of Gomera. This place is small, with a hundred inhabitants more or less, and a church, which is good for such a place, situated on level ground between two very high hills. I confessed and took the holy sacrament, and afterwards rested and amused myself for two days. I also enjoyed the cooling drinks which were made by a slave girl, who was an excellent cook, for my own people did not know how to make them. We then continued our voyage, but a servant from Seville left me here, dreading the sea voyage, and I got another in his place.

## XXXVI.

WHAT HAPPENED TO ME ON THE OCEAN, WHICH EXTENDS FOR A THOU-
SAND LEAGUES FROM THE PORT OF GOMERA TO SAN DOMINGO IN
THE INDIES.

It is now ten days since we have seen land, and we shall consider ourselves lucky if we see it in twenty days from this time. Fortunate are they who now sit down content before their fresh roast meat, especially if a fountain of water flows near their doors. They have now begun to serve out water to us by a measure, and the people on board prefer drinking what is in the ship, to seeing that which is outside. I really believe that there are many here who would be glad to return to Spain, and to have paid their passages without making the voyage. Three other vessels sail with us, in company.

This sea, though sometimes enraged and made furious by the winds, which move it according to the will of God, without which a single leaf could not fall from a tree, is yet generally more smooth than other seas. Some say that the cause of this is that it is very large, and that there is more space for the waters, which are not confined by coasts where they are stopped and impeded. There are fish that they call flying fish, which fly for twenty paces, more or less, and sometimes fall on board the ship. I saw and ate some, which had a smoky taste : I do not know whether this was caused by the smoke in which they were roasted, or whether it was natural. Those that I saw were about a span long, with a broad tail, two fins near the head an inch in breadth, and wings the size of those of a bat.

## XXXVII.

### WHAT HAPPENED DURING THE VOYAGE TO THE INDIES.

As I left Spain a banished man, in disgrace with the Emperor; and as I am naturally of a quarrelsome as well as a merry disposition, I determined, in order to avoid the chance of suffering as I had formerly done, to disarm both myself and my followers, and thus I mixed with the sailor lads as one of themselves. I ate their salt fish with them, on my knees, and allowed them to share my fowls ; because

M

I thought I might benefit by their speaking well of me, and that they would report my peaceful and jovial conduct on their return to Seville. One morning, when I rose from my cot, and came on deck, I found the captain of the ship with a sword by his side, which he had not worn until now, and several men armed with darts on the main topsail yard. I said to the captain, " O great Captain, what is the matter?" He replied that several French ships were reported to be in these seas, coming from Brazil, and that he wished to be found ready for them, and not to be caught like a pig. I was amused, and called to my lads to bring me my sword, and to get theirs. He replied, very haughtily, that I must do no such thing, for that he had been watching me, and had seen cause to suspect that I wanted to seize the ship, for that I could have no other motive for making the sailor lads my companions and equals.

I answered: " Sir, you may make your mind easy, for I swear by God, and by my habit of the order of Santiago, that you may sleep in peace and have pleasant dreams, for I have no such intention. Free yourself, good Captain, from this delusion." He said that he was not satisfied, for that he had been told that I intended to cut the halliard, which is the rope that supports the mainsail, and to kill him, and all his friends. I soon saw that no one had told him this, but that he had invented it to conceal his folly and to hide his fear. All that I did to assure him he took offence at; and there was a great commotion in the ship, but at last he was pacified.

We continued our voyage until we came in sight of some islands, one of which is called Anguila; another, Sombrero;[1] a third, Anegada;[2] and some others, the Virgin

[1] Sombrero is a rock near St. Thomas's, the first land which is sighted by the West India packets, in their voyage from Southampton to that island.

[2] Anegada is a dangerous reef, a little to the westward of the Sombrero rock.

Islands. From the Canary islands to these islands, we had gone eight hundred leagues over the sea, suffering hunger and thirst, and seeing no land for twenty-five days. We came to an anchor off one of these islands, which are in the Indies, and inhabited by fierce and warlike men, called Carribs. They fight with each other; and when they take or kill their enemies, they eat them. If the prisoner they capture is thin, they make a hole in the ground, and fatten him in it, and afterwards eat him. The hands and feet are considered the most dainty morsels, and these they give to those whom they desire to please. These Carribs are fierce, and can defend themselves with arrows; and, as their land does not yield gold, the Christians have passed it on one side, and pressed on; and we did so also, coming to off an island inhabited by Christians, called San Juan de Puerto Rico.

Puerto Rico is a fertile island, containing two large Christian towns, called Puerto Rico and San German. The distance between one and the other is twenty leagues by land, and a day and a half's voyage by sea from Puerto Rico to Son German, but at least a month's voyage from San German to Puerto Rico. There are many fruits in the island: some called *batatas ;*[1] others, *ajïs ;*[2] others, *piñas ;*[3] others, *pitahayas ;*[4] others, *guayavas ;*[5] others, *mamayas ;*[6] others, *cocoços ;*[7] others, *platanas ;*[8] but the only fruits which have been introduced from Spain are citrons, oranges, melons, cucumbers, lettuce, cauliflowers, pomegranates, and figs. There is a fish here called *manati*, the size of a bullock, and tasting like veal; and it comes out of the sea to browse on land. It looks like a calf in the face, but its eyes are smaller, resembling those of a goshawk. These beasts are

---

[1] *Convolvulus Batatas.* Sweet potato.
[2] A capsicum.
[3] Pine apples.
[4] Pitajaiæ Cactus.
[5] Guavas.
[6] The Mamay apple.
[7] Cocoa nut ?
[8] Plantains.

very fat, and the flesh is eaten roasted with sauce. If a man did not see the *manati* taken out of the water, he would think the flesh was that of a bullock, especially after it is cooked. I am sure that there is no good Christian who, if he did not know beforehand, would not think he was eating beef, even if they assured him that it was fish. I also saw turtles of the size of large wheels, and these also taste like meat. In this island there are no flies, no lice, no fleas, no bugs, and no water lizards, nor other evil insects; but there are rats and great land lizards. There are plenty of sheep and cattle, and several gold mines. All the Indians are either dead, or have escaped from the island, except a few whom the Christians retain as slaves.

We were here for eleven days. I found many sons of servants of my ancestors, especially of the family of Medina Sidonia, who received me with much honour, and entertained me with bull fights, and tilting matches. The water is very good, though it is brought from a distance of about half a league from the town. In this town of Puerto Rico there is a very good church, and a monastery of Dominican friars, who are very devout. The monastery and church are built of stone and mortar, and roofed with tiles; but all the houses, except one or two, have their walls and the floors of the upper stories of wood, and the roofs of tiles. There are between four and five hundred inhabitants, and they all have very good houses in the country, which they call *estancias*. We sailed from Puerto Rico to the island of Española.

----

## XXXVIII.

I arrived in the island of Española, and came to a town called Santo Domingo. The island is fertile, and abounds in all that the world can produce. The town is built on a plain, and consists of many good houses, both of brick and stone. The fields are green all the year round, and the land is never bare, nor do the leaves ever fall from the trees. This is the reason that corn and the vine will not thrive, but they are brought in abundance by traders, as well as every other needful article; indeed the wine is better here than in Portugal, because the sea voyage improves it. The earth yields abundantly, and as soon as one harvest is got in another is reaped, so that there are two every year. The city is very near a large river where ships enter, and the water is so deep that they put planks from the ships to the shore, to unload the cargos.

I disembarked at this port, and Diego Caballero, Secretary to the Royal Audience, took me to his lodgings, and he required no witnesses to prove my lineage and condition, for he was a discreet man and a fellow townsman. He lodged and treated me as if I had been the Constable of Castile, and I did not enjoy his society more than he did mine; so that I consider his friendship as a great piece of good fortune. The President and Judges of this Royal Audience had received orders from the Emperor to provide for the office of Captain-General of the province of Santa Martha; and, having received strong recommendations from the Secretary, representing my fitness, the President assembled the Judges, namely, the Licentiate      ¹ of Segovia, and the Doctor Ynfante of Seville, and appointed me to the office of Captain-General, giving me the following Royal Commission:

" Don Carlos, etc.: inasmuch as, for reasons connected with our royal service, we have commissioned and ordered the Doctor Rodrigo Ynfante, a Judge of our Royal Audience in the island of Española, to proceed to the province of Santa Martha as ' Juez de Residencia'² to take the ' Resi-

¹ Illegible in MS.
² At the expiration of the term of office of all Spanish governors,

dencia' of Garcia de Lerma, formerly our Governor in the said Province, and to take charge of the administration of judges, and their subordinates, a "Juez de residencia" was appointed to examine into their conduct, and receive complaints and representations from those whom they had governed or judged. This was called a *residencia* or *visita*. Solorzano, in his *Politica Indiana*, states the intention of this institution to be the furnishing of a motive for attention and zeal on the part of the officials, and the prevention of all excesses and acts of insolence which might otherwise frequently take place, especially in the remote provinces of the Indies. The *residencia* was thus intended to serve as a bridle and check to bad, and a source of encouragement to good ministers.

But Solorzano points out many evils in the working of this system. At the approach of the time of the *residencia* the governors became terrified, and the people were apt to treat them with disrespect, so that they feared to administer justice with that freedom which is essential. Then again, on the arrival of the "Juez de residencia," the scum of society, the envious, the perjured, and the disappointed, poured in a shower of accusations which were often frivolous and vexatious. The Marquis of Montes Claros, who was Viceroy of Peru from 1607 to 1615, compared these *residencias* to the eddies in the corners of streets on a windy day, which only serve to raise the dust and bits of straw over the heads of the passengers. Thus, conscientious and upright governors were often in more danger from the proceedings of the "Juez de residencia" than extortioners and receivers of bribes. The former, secure in the consciousness of right, took no pains to silence the tongues of their enemies; while the latter, "wiser in their generation than the children of light," as the expiration of their term of office approached, made friends even of those whom they had injured.

Another great evil of the *residencias* in the Indies, was their long duration. They often lasted eighteen or twenty years, and the *residencia* of the Marquis of Villa Manrique, Viceroy of Mexico, which was entrusted to the Bishop of Tlascala, never came to an end at all. Compared with these interminable proceedings, the persecution of Warren Hastings for seven years, by his "Juez de residencia," Edmund Burke, was a mere trifle. Solarzano complained of this great evil. He thought that three or four years ought to be amply sufficient for the *residencia* even of a Judge of the Audencia of Lima or Mexico ; and remarked that "the Prince will not perfectly cure his commonwealth with this medicine, if the medicine brings with it greater evils than those which it is intended to remedy."

On the whole, however, these *residencias*, with all their faults, were a wholesome check on the rapacity and mal-administration of the Spanish officials in South Amerioa. See *Politica Indiana de Dr. Don Juan de Solorzano*. Lib. v, cap. x, pp. 836-49.

justice until otherwise provided for; and, as we have received intelligence from numerous persons in our Council of the Indies, and as it is notorious that the said province is in a disturbed state, with many Indian Caciques in rebellion; therefore, to remedy these evils, it is decreed that a body of men shall be sent to people and restore peace to the said province." " The President and Judges of the Royal Audience having seen and considered these commands, find that at present there are many people in this island of Española who desire to go to Tierra Firme and to the provinces of Peru, and they have resolved to send some of these people to the said province of Santa Martha. They also, hereby, appoint Don Alonzo Enriquez de Guzman to go as Captain General of the said people, he being a Knight of the Order of Santiago, and Gentleman of the Royal Household. He will proceed in the conquest and settlement of the country, in concert with Dr. Ynfante, our ' Juez de Residencia;' and we command the officers, who may be appointed, to obey him as their Captain General. Given in Santo Domingo, on the 12th of December, 1534.

Having received this appointment of Captain General in the island of Española, I appointed my officers and bought horses and all other necessaries. I was on the point of embarking for Santa Martha, when a ship arrived from Spain with the news that the Emperor had appointed Don Pedro de Lugo, Adelantado of the Canary Islands, to be Captain General of the said province of Santa Martha, who, with his son Don Luis de Lugo,[1] and five hundred soldiers, might shortly be expected. I was, therefore, obliged to resign my appointment, and I then determined to go to Peru, a newly discovered land, where there is an infinite quantity of gold. But the gold cannot be obtained for nothing, eighty men dying out of a hundred who go to Peru. This

[1] See my introduction to the *Expedition of Pedro de Ursua*, etc., p. x and xi, printed for the Hakluyt Society.

reminds me of the physician of the King of England, who
was told that if he effected a cure he should receive a city,
and that if not he should be hanged. It is very certain that
a great prize is never gained at small cost.

## XXXIX.

### HOW I CROSSED THE ISTHMUS OF PANAMA.

I sailed from the island of Española on my way to Peru,
and arrived at the port of Nombre de Dios, in the province
of Castilla del Oro. The native name of the place means
*Bones*, and it was so called on account of the number of
people who have died here. Of the six horses which I
landed at this port, I sold three, and sent three by land to
Panama, a port on the shores of the South Sea. I travelled
across the land to Panama, a distance of eighteen leagues.
For the first seven the road passes between two high ranges
of hills, densely covered with forest, along the banks of a
river which was nearly dry, the water reaching to the hocks
of the horses, but in some places to the girths; and, to those
who travel on foot, it is a very weary journey. For the
last eleven leagues the road is better, though there are
several rivers to pass. There are three inns on the road,
one called Capira, the second La Junta, and the third La
Venta de Chagres,[1] because here they disembark from
another deep river called Chagres.

I must now tell you what I saw in this province of Castilla del Oro, and what I thought of the Indians, and afterwards, if I live, I will tell you about Peru.

The Indian people appeared to me to be like what we
should have been, if Adam had never sinned. They neither

[1] This is probably the place now called Barbacoas, where the railway
bridge crosses the river Chagres.

sin, nor know how to sin; they feel neither envy nor
malice; they have no money amongst them, nor do they
require any; and, as to clothing, they go about as their
mothers bore them, excepting a small cotton cloth between
the legs. They are very timorous respecting all things in
the world, excepting death, for they know not that there is
any other world either for rewards or punishments. They
are very loyal, and will suffer floggings, tortures, and
death before they will say a word which might do harm to
their masters or their country.

In this land of Panama there are many parrots as large as
crows, tigers, turtles, and animals called *yguanas*, the size of
large cats, which are very good to eat, as well as their eggs,
of which they each have twenty or thirty. There are also
wild pigs in the forests, somewhat smaller than those in
Castile, with their navels on their backs. I say this,
because I have seen them; for I shall tell no lies, because I
must give an account to God of what you may here read.
There are bats which, when they succeed in finding any part
of a man uncovered, suck the blood until he dies. The land
is very fertile and densely wooded, and the reason of this is
partly because the people neither sow nor gather in harvests,
and partly because the rains are very heavy. It is always
very hot, and there is no cold either in winter or summer.
The bread is made from roots, and they take very little
trouble either in sowing or gathering them, using no iron
tools, but merely working with poles and by hand; thus the
people can live without much labour, if we would leave
them alone.

To sail in the South Sea is like navigating a smooth river
without wind. December, January, February, and March
are the best seasons for navigating. I sailed from Panama
on the 20th of March, with three horses, the passage costing
me four hundred and fifty *castellanos de oro* for the horses,
twenty for my slaves, and one hundred for my own passage

N

and for my cabin, with very good ship's stores. Two days before I embarked in this port of Panama, I received a letter from a very good friend of mine, advising me to return, saying that I wanted more wealth than was reasonable, seeing that I had 150,000 maravedis of rent, and that I ought not to go in search of more.

## XL.

### HOW I ARRIVED IN THE LAND OF PERU.

I shall not tell you so much of what I saw, as of what happened to me, because I have already told you that this book is a record of my adventures. I arrived in the bay of San Mateo, in the land of Peru, in the end of March, and there I disembarked the horses and part of the people, who went by land to a point called Santa Elena, where they were re-embarked, and conveyed to Tumbez.

I reached a port called Puerto Viejo, in the South Sea, and in the land of Peru, where all my hardships and dangers commenced. This voyage over the South Sea is troublesome, on account of the delays caused by the light winds. I disembarked the horses after much difficulty, and gave thanks to our Lord and Saviour that I had been able to get them safely on shore. As I did not require more than one for myself, and another for my page, who carried my spear and knapsack, I determined to sell my third horse to an officer named Garces, for a thousand *pesos de oro*, at four hundred and fifty maravedis each, and seventy marcs of fine silver. Afterwards one of my own horses died, and I bought another for a thousand *castellanos de oro*. Though I bought the horse dear, I gave thanks, because in other things, as well as regards my own health as those of my servants, I was fortunate; and of this evil accident I said, " you come well if you come alone." From Tumbez the distance is thirty leagues by land to San Miguel, a place which is fifteen leagues from the port where ships usually anchor; and they did not build the town at the port, because there is neither wood nor water there.

## XLI.

### OF THE INDIANS OF PERU, AND OF ATABALIPA, WHO WAS KILLED BY THE SPANIARDS.

The Indians of this land of Peru are a gentle and peaceful people, living on such light food as gourds and *batatas*,[1] cooked with a sort of spice called *aji*,[2] which they use in all their dishes. Occasionally they eat meat and fish. The meat is from a strange kind of sheep, which can go without eating for fifteen days. The chief of these Indians was Atabalipa,[3] who, as I have been told by many witnesses, only wanted Christianity to make him worthy of being a king. There are not so many ants in Spain as there are Indians in this country. This Atabalipa, when he was taken prisoner and put to death by the Spaniards, was about thirty years of age, of middle height, somewhat fat, with a round fair face, and the manners of a gentleman. He was served by women and not by men; and he wore a fringe on his forehead, in the manner of a crown. No one approached him without bringing a present in token of submission; and, though those who came were great nobles, they entered with the present on their own backs, and without shoes. He was carried on men's shoulders when travelling, and roads were made five hundred leagues long, and broad enough to allow ten horses to ride abreast, the ground being as smooth as the palm of the hand, with a wall on each side, and trees in

---

[1] Sweet potatoes.    [2] A species of capsicum.    [3] Atahualpa.

double rows to keep off the sun. Atabalipa was so intelligent, that in twenty days he understood the language of the christians, and learnt to play at chess and at cards. He was the son of a great king of a province called Cuzco, and of another called Quito, named Guaynacapa,[1] who reigned over more than fifteen hundred leagues of country. This king was loved and served as if he had been God himself; they adored him as a God when alive, and believe the same now that he is dead. He had two sons, namely this Atabalipa and another, who was the eldest, to whom he gave the kingdom of Cuzco, while Quito was given to Atabalipa. After the father died, the sons fought for the sovereignty, and Atabalipa sent one of his captains with a great army against Cuzco, where a battle was fought and the brother was taken prisoner; and thus Atabalipa was king of Cuzco as well as of Quito.

He marched with a great army, establishing his authority through the country, until the arrival of the Christians caused him to return. He did not come to fight them, but rather to chastise them for the harm they were doing in his country; and thus he was ruined through despising his enemy, for otherwise he could not have been captured. He was taken, and put to death in the following manner. The Christians arrived within a league and a half of the Indian army, and they then sent ten men on horseback to say that they wanted not their gold nor their silver, nor to do them any injury, nor to subjugate them; but that they only wished to be their friends and brothers. These envoys tried to frighten the Indians with their horses, which caused much terror to men who had never seen such animals before; and they forced their horses' heads over the head of Atabalipa, when he was sitting in state, so that the breath from their nostrils moved the fringe on his forehead. The Spaniards were astonished that, though he had never seen horses before, he

---

[1] Huayna Capac.

was not in the least terrified, nor did he even raise his head; but he heard what they had to say, and replied that if the Christians desired to be the friends and brothers of the Indians, they should return all the gold they had robbed from his vassals at Tumbez: he also said that he desired their friendship, and that he would visit them on another day.

Accordingly, he came with a great multitude of people, and a friar[1] came out to receive him with the commandments of the Christian faith, which many of us do not know as well as we ought, and, telling Atabalipa that the book contained the decrees of God, he put it into his hand. Atabalipa took it, and threw it on the ground, saying—" I neither understand, nor do I desire to understand, what you say; but you have robbed my vassals; and when you have returned to them their silver and gold, I will be your brother and friend." Then the rascally friar, who was certainly a peace breaker, began to call with a loud voice, saying—"Christians! I call upon you to avenge this insult to the faith of Jesus Christ." The soldiers obeyed, killed a great number of the Indians, and imprisoned Atabalipa.

During the two months that elapsed between his capture and his death Atabalipa learnt many things. He was much astonished at the way in which the Christians communicated with each other by writing; and he acted in a very different way from the other king who was captured by Hernando Cortes in New Spain, who believed that the letter spoke, and asked it to say to him what it had said to the Christians. On the contrary, Atabalipa asked a man to write down certain words which he knew, and afterwards went aside and asked another man to read them; and thus he learnt to understand these marvels. He inquired of the Captain Pizarro if he was the King of the Christians, and Pizarro replied that he was one of the least of the knights out of the innumerable number who served the Emperor. Atabalipa

[1] The fanatical Vincente de Valverde, afterwards Bishop of Cuzco.

then asked how many men the Emperor could bring into the field, and was told 500,000.

One day the Captain Pizarro told him that he was a gentleman. He replied angrily that he was such as his mother had borne him; but that if the Spaniards would release him, he would fill a room with gold, twenty-five feet square and fifty feet high. Pizarro said that he was content, and the gold was brought; but afterwards Pizarro condemned Atabalipa to be burnt. Atabalipa then said that if he wanted more gold he would provide it, but that it would be wiser to keep him alive in prison, where he could order his vassals not to oppose the Christians, than to kill him. And he spoke the truth; for after they killed him, the Indians killed many Christians, and even now the country is not safe. They, however, took him out to burn him; and the three hundred women who attended upon him followed him weeping. Among them were twenty of his sisters; and they could not separate them from him until he was strangled. The tears came into his eyes; and when they asked the cause, he said that it was because they were killing him without reason. God, who knows all things, visible and invisible, will be the judge of this act; but I, for my sins, am only able to judge of that which is visible. Atabalipa died a Christian, and received the water of baptism; and if he did not benefit by it in this world, his soul will yet be received into glory.

---

## XLII.

I ARRIVE AT PIURA, IN THE PROVINCE OF PERU, AND AFTERWARDS GO
TO THE CITY OF KINGS.

I arrived at a city in Peru, inhabited by Christians, which is called Piura, fifteen leagues from the port[1] where I had disembarked. They did not build the town on

[1] Payta.

the sea-shore, because there is neither water, nor wood, nor grass for the horses.   The Judge and Regidores[1] of the town sent me all kinds of refreshments when I was three leagues off, and my entrance took place at sunset, as they had arranged.  They came out for a league to meet me; and thus I entered the town, where I was very well lodged, and enabled to recover from the fatigues of the voyage, as well as my servants and horses.

The great city of Tumbez is inhabited entirely by Indians. It is on the sea-shore; and in it there is a great house, belonging to the lord of the country, with walls built of adobes,[2] like bricks, very beautifully painted with many colours, and varnished, so that I never saw anything more beautiful.  The roof is of straw, also painted, so that it looks like gold, very strong, and very handsome.[3]

The distance from this place to Cuzco is three hundred leagues, and along the whole way there is a straight smooth road, passing amongst very lofty naked mountains, bare of grass or trees.  On the coast there is an infinite quantity of sand, and when the wind raises it, it looks like clouds of snow.  The road is bounded on each side by walls, two yards thick, and six in height.  In some parts there are rows of trees which yield a fruit like that of the carob tree. Every three, or at most every four leagues, there is a house which the Indians call tambo, but which we, in Spain, should call an inn.  These tambos are well built, for the use of the lord of the land when he travels from the great city of Cuzco to Tumbez.  I have already said that this Lord was called Guaynacapa, and that he was the father of Atabalipa.

Seventy leagues from Piura, and near the sea coast, there is a city which, in the language of the Indians, is called Chimu, and by the Spaniards Truxillo.  Another eighty

---

[1] Magistrates.            [2] Huge bricks baked in the sun.
[3] For an account of Tumbez, before its destruction by the Spaniards, see Prescott's Conquest of Peru, i, p. 256.

leagues further on, there is another city inhabited by Christians, two leagues from the sea shore, called by the Indians
Lima, and in our language, the City of the Kings.    Here I
arrived very tired, with swollen ankles.[1]   I was cured by a
woman who was married, honest, and ugly; and she sug-
gested to me the following reflections.   He who is not married, should not seek for a pretty woman, but for an ugly
one, for the following reasons.   First, because the ugly
woman is free from two inconveniences, namely, annoyance
from the attentions of other men, and from the love of her
own husband; for he knows that, as she has no other re-
source, she must love him, and therefore gives her no trouble.   But the pretty woman loves her husband for the first
year, and runs after other men all the rest of her life; who
have more use of her than her own husband.

## XLIII.

WHAT HAPPENED TO ME IN THE PRINCIPAL CITY OF PERU, WHICH IS
    NOW CALLED THE CITY OF KINGS, AND OF MY FIRST INTERVIEW
    WITH HIS LORDSHIP THE GOVERNOR.

I arrived in the city which is called Lima in the language
of the Indians, and in our language the City of the Kings,
which is laid out on a regular plan, with gardens and houses.
The Infidels, or, as they ought more truly to be called, the
Innocents, of this country, live in huts made of canes, like
places where poultry roost, for in this country it is neither
hot nor cold, and it never rains.   I mean on the coast, for
in the mountains, which are very near, there is another
world of snow and ice and rain.   Now the Spaniards have

---

[1] He seems to have travelled over the whole distance from Piura to
Lima, by the sandy deserts of the coast.

built themselves houses of *adobes*, handsomely painted and finished like those in Spain, with good gardens behind them.

When I approached the city, the Regidores came out to meet me, for the Governor had not yet arrived from the great city of Cuzco. All the respectable people came out to meet me, numbering forty-six on horseback, including the chamberlain of the Governor, who had charge of the fine palaces and houses which had recently been built. He said that his master had ordered him to lodge me in his own house, where I remained until the arrival of the Governor.

At this time I was suffering from a most dreadful toothache, and as the object of this book is to relate all the troubles I had to encounter, I will first tell you how I cured the toothache, and afterwards I will relate what passed between the Governor and myself.

To cure the toothache take some *aji*, which we call Indian pepper, and apply it to the tooth; then put some hot olive oil on a cloth, and squeeze it over the place. This pain is so common and yet so terrible, that a remedy for it is almost as valuable as a remedy for loss of life or honour.

The Governor, Don Francisco Pizarro, received me very honourably, and, on the following day, he sent me a thousand *castellanos*, to pay my travelling expenses.[1]  Soon afterwards he said to me: " Sir, I desired to promote you to a post according to your merits, and I regret that I have none better to give you, than the one to which I have appointed you; but in the interior there is much land to conquer, in the performance of which good service will be rendered to God, and to our lord the King." I gave him thanks, and

---

[1] Don Alonzo arrived at Lima shortly after the interview between Almagro and Pizarro at Cuzco, which led to a solemn agreement, dated June 12, 1535, by which the two conquerors bound themselves to preserve their friendship inviolate, and to divide the profits of all future conquests. Almagro then set out to discover Chile, while Pizarro returned to Lima, where he found Don Alonzo.

accepted his offer, being rejoiced to have the means of serving God and the King, by encountering so many hardships and dangers by sea and land, by rivers and mountains, in hunger and in thirst.   At this time I sent a letter to the Secretary Don Francisco de los Cobos, Commander of Leon, of the order of Santiago ; which was as follows :

" Illustrious Sir,

" Ever since you have known me, I have been poor in estate but rich in judgment; wanting the former, as much as I abounded in the latter.   I now desire that you will inform his Majesty that I am working in his service, and I beseech you to explain this fully to the King my master."

## XLIV.

HOW I DEPARTED FROM THIS CITY, WHICH IS CALLED LIMA IN THE
LANGUAGE OF THE INDIANS, AND BY US THE CITY OF KINGS; AND
CAME TO THE GREAT CITY OF CUZCO, WHICH WAS THE SEAT OF
THE LORD OF THE COUNTRY, AND THE PLACE WHERE THE HOUSE
OF THE SUN WAS BUILT ; FOR THE INDIANS BELIEVE THE SUN TO
BE GOD.

I set out from the City of Kings well supplied with horses, servants, and provisions, and the distance to Cuzco is one hundred and thirty leagues over the most rugged mountains that can possibly be imagined.   The object of my journey was the conquest of a province called Chiriguana,[1] which I was unable to effect, as you will presently see, owing to the rising of the Indians.

I arrived at this city of Cuzco, tired and worn out by the

[1] The Chiriguanas are a tribe of Indians inhabiting a part of the " Gran Chacu" in the Eastern and forest covered portion of the modern Republic of Bolivia.   When the Inca Yupanqui conquered them they were cannibals, and in 1571 they repulsed an invasion of Spaniards, led by the Viceroy Don Francisco de Toledo in person.

long and rugged road, and the difficulty of getting provisions; for we had to take what we wanted from the Indians, and they killed one of my slaves, who had cost me six hundred *castellanos*. This city is built in a valley, and the houses are very lofty, with walls of hewn stone, strongly and beautifully worked. At a distance of three casts of a sling from the city, near some very high hills, there is a great fortress, which is no less beautiful than strong, all of quarried stone. The Indians have a youth of twenty years, a little more or less, for king, named Capa-ynga,[1] which means, in our language, sole lord. He succeeded after Atabalipa, his brother, both being sons of Guaynacapa, who had a hundred sons and fifty daughters. The Indians adored this Guaynacapa, saying that he was a child of the sun; and they also worship his son Capa-ynga. These people have the following custom. At the age of fifteen years they bore the ears of all their children; and this ceremony takes place every year, with the same solemnity as is observed in admitting to holy orders in Spain. On these occasions the youths promise three things—to worship the sun, to serve Capa-ynga, and to sow maize, which is their bread.

The Spaniards ill-treated the caciques and Indians, overworking them, burning them, and tormenting them for gold and silver; and one day Capa-ynga, on pretence of seeking for gold for Hernando Pizarro, the brother of the governor, who was at that time acting as his lieutenant at Cuzco, left the city and never returned. He raised the country against us, and collected 50,000 armed men, the Christians not numbering more than two hundred, half of them being lame or halt. One day the Indians entered the city in the morning, by seven different points, fighting so fiercely, and burning as they advanced, that they gained half the city, and there was

[1] Manco Inca. He was a son of the great monarch Inca Huayna Ceapac.

little left to burn, because the houses were thatched with straw.

God, and some force of our own, assisted us; but, in addition to the numbers and ferocity of the Indians, the smoke was so dense that we could not see each other. The conflict lasted from the morning of one day to the morning of the next. With the aid of God we at length drove the Indians back towards the fortress, where there was a captain of Capa-ynga, who was called Villa-uma.[1] He was their Pope, and had charge of the house of the sun. We then assaulted and captured the fortress, killing 3,000 Indians; and they killed our captain, Juan Pizarro, a brother of the governor, a youth aged twenty-five years, and possessed of 200,000 ducats in money. During the combat in the city the Indians killed four Christians, besides more than thirty whom they killed in the farms of caciques, who were out collecting tribute.

I accepted the office of maestro del campo because I was asked and importuned to undertake it, and they gave me Rodrigo de Pineda,[2] as my lieutenant, who was a nephew of Juan de Pineda, secretary to the municipality of Seville. This was my reason for abandoning my previous intention of undertaking the service to which I was appointed by the Governor Francisco Pizarro.[3]

The Indians of Cuzco are better dressed than those of any of the other provinces, both because it is colder here in winter, and because the land is more fertile, and the people are richer. They are much afraid of our horses, but their

[1] Huillac-umu, or high-priest of the sun. Most accounts state that this dignitary accompanied Almagro in his expedition to Chile.

[2] Rodrigo de Pineda afterwards settled in Cuzco. In 1552 he was forced, as a citizen of that town, through fear of ill-treatment, to join Francisco Hernandez Giron in his rebellion; and that rebel made him a captain of cavalry. Pineda deserted to the royal army, under the Marshal Alvarado, on the first opportunity.

[3] Namely, the conquest of Chiriguana. See ante, p. 98.

mountains offer an excellent means of defence against them. They have no defensive, but many offensive arms, such as lances, arrows, clubs, axes, halberds, darts, and slings, and another weapon which they call *ayllas*, consisting of three round stones sewn up in leather, and each fastened to a cord a cubit long. They throw these at the horses, and thus bind their legs together; and sometimes they will fasten a man's arms to his sides in the same way. These Indians are so expert in the use of this weapon that they will bring down a deer with it in the chase. Their principal weapon, however, is the sling, which I have delayed mentioning to the last. With it they will hurl a huge stone with such force that it will kill a horse; in truth, the effect is little less great than that of an arquebus; and I have seen a stone, thus hurled from a sling, break a sword in two pieces, which was held in a man's hand at a distance of thirty paces. The Indians also adopted the following stratagem : they made an endless number of deep holes, with stakes bristling in them, and covered over with straw and earth. The horses often fell into them; and the rider was generally killed.

I am able to certify that this was the most fearful and cruel war in the world; for between the Christians and Moors there is some fellow-feeling, and both sides follow their own interests in sparing those whom they take alive, for the sake of their ransoms; but in this Indian war there is no such feeling on one side or the other, and they give each other the most cruel deaths they can invent. After this there happened many things, which I remit to the chronicler who may hereafter write upon this subject.[1]

[1] It is very provoking that Don Alonzo should not have written a more detailed account of the siege of Cuzco, the most interesting event in the history of the conquest of Peru. See *Prescott*, vol. ii, chap. x ; *Helps*, vol. iv, book xvii, chap. iii ; *G. de la Vega, Comm. Real.*, pt. ii, lib. ii, cap. xxiv ; *Herrera*, dec. iv, lib. ii, cap. iii, etc., etc., etc.

## XLV.

### OF THE GOVERNOR, FRANCISCO PIZARRO.

At this time, and in this land, I received letters from my relations, and among them there was one from the best friend I have in the whole world, who is Don Pedro Enriquez de Ribera,[1] nephew and heir to the very illustrious Lord Don Fadrique Enriquez de Ribera, who had no children. He expressed a strong desire to see me again; and to please him, no less than to see my honoured wife, I determined to leave this rich though rugged land, and to return to my own. I procured, as a present for Don Pedro Enriquez, a precious vase of gold, with jewels round the rim, and a fine plume of feathers; and for Don Fadrique, his brother, who is an equally virtuous and honourable knight, I got a beautiful fish, with a drinking vessel on the top, all made of silver.

Although it was my intention and desire to leave this land

[1] This knight appears to have been Don Alonzo's most intimate friend, and he mentions him on several other occasions (see pages 46 to 50, 66, etc.) The founder of the Ribera family was Don Perafan de Ribera, hereditary Adelantado of Andalusia, in the time of Alonzo XI, who was killed in a battle with the Moors near Algeziras. His great granddaughter and heiress Catalina, Countess of Molar, married Don Pedro Enriquez, Lord of Tarifa, a scion of the house of Enriquez, Admirals of Castile. They had two sons, Fadrique and Fernando. Don Fadrique, fifth Count of Molar and first Marquis of Tarifa, went to Jerusalem and died without male issue. His brother Fernando, a native of Seville, married Inez de Portocarrero, and had three sons, Pedro, our author's friend, Fadrique, and Fernando. Don Pedro Enriquez de Ribera succeeded his uncle as Count of Molar, Marquis of Tarifa, and Adelantado of Andalusia. He served, under Philip II, as Viceroy of Catalonia, and afterwards of Naples. In 1588 he was created Duke of Alcala; but he had no legitimate children. He had a natural son Juan, Bishop of Badajos, Archbishop of Valencia, and Patriarch of Alexandria. His brother Fernando succeeded him as second Duke of Alcala, and married Juana, a daughter of Hernan Cortes, the conqueror of Mexico, from whom the Dukes of Alcala descend.

in December 1536, and go to that in which I was born, yet it was not the will of God that I should do so at once, because all the roads were closed, and the whole country was in arms. These Indians, not content with keeping us eight months so that no one could learn what had become of us, came every month, in a body numbering at least 70,000, to try our defences. I, however, kept my gold and silver ready, waiting for the time when it should please God to open the road for us.

It was my intention not to put any more letters into this book, but I shall give one more, because it is short and worthy of note; so I trust you will pardon me. It is from the Adelantado Don Francisco Pizarro, Governor of this new land, which in Spain we call Peru, though here they have a different name. The letter was as follows:—

" Magnificent Sir,—To-day I arrived at this City of the Kings, from a visit to the cities of San Miguel and Truxillo, with the intention of resting after so many dangers and labours; but before I could put my feet to the ground, they gave me letters from your worship, and from my brothers, in which I am informed of the rebellion of this traitor, the ynga. This has caused me much concern, both on account of the detriment it will cause to the service of the Emperor our lord, of the dangers in which you are placed, and of the trouble it will cause me in my old age. I am consoled by your presence at Cuzco, and, if it be the will of God, we will send succour; and thus I leave you, praying our Lord to guard your magnificent person. This 4th of May, 1536.

" FRANCISCO PIZARRO."

This Francisco Pizarro was a knight, the son of another very honourable knight of Truxillo in Estremadura. His mother was a native of San Lucar, four leagues from Seville in Andalusia, of which I am a native; and as he was of a noble family, he desired to live prosperously, and passed

over to the Indies, where he laboured until at last he
achieved his desire, after many strange adventures, and
became Adelantado and Governor of this rich land, thus
doing good service to the Emperor our lord.   But neither
prosperity, nor riches, nor the favour of the Emperor made
him so proud as to cease to be a good Christian and a good
companion, without pomps and vanities.   He was much be-
loved by the people whom he governed, for he was very
friendly and affable, and very loyal to his king and lord.

## XLVI.

### HOW THE VIRGIN MARY HELPED US ON HER HOLY DAY.

I do not desire that what our Lady the Virgin Mary,
Mother of God, did for us on her own holy day, which falls
on the 8th of September, thus strengthening our faith,
should remain unknown.   We had been besieged in this
city of Cuzco for five months, by 100,000 men, who had
often attacked us, and burnt the city, so that we were
obliged to live in tents in the *plaza,* and they had also killed
the brother of our governor and many other Christians.   All
this time we knew nothing of the governor, who was one hundred and fifty leagues from us, and we believed him to be dead;
and it was proposed that out of our number of one hundred and
fifty fighting men, the best fifty with the best horses should
be sent to find out the fate of the governor, and to ascertain
the reason that he had not sent us succour.   They disputed
much over this proposal; to some it seemed good, and to
others evil, but at last it was determined to send them.   It
was then that the Mother of God interfered, on her holy day;
for after mass, being the day before they were to set out,
many Indians in the surrounding hills raised a loud shout.
The Captain Hernando Pizarro sallied forth to attack them,

and found five heads of Christians in the road, and more than a thousand letters. The Indians had seized these Christians, whom the governor had sent to us, and killed them; and they had thrown their heads in the road that we might know it, and thus be disheartened. But, on the contrary, this animated us and gave us new life; and the event took place on our Lady's holy day, so we determined not to divide our force. For by these letters we learnt what we desired to know, that the governor was alive, and also that the emperor had gained a victory in Barbary, and captured Tunis. My letters also reached me in this way, both those from my native land, and the above letter from the governor.

## XLVII.

### DIEGO ALMAGRO ARRIVES IN CUZCO.

Though I have before stated that the number of Indians who besieged us amounted to 100,000, yet others say there were 300,000, for these Indians are great liars. The Adelantado Diego de Almagro, who took a principal part in the conquest of these kingdoms, desired to complete it, though only with one eye, as the other had been put out by an arrow. He had marched eight hundred and fifty leagues beyond this city of Cuzco with five hundred men, all of them of gentle birth. This Diego de Almagro, both from the gallantry of his person, his liberality, and his loyalty to his King, may be compared to the Cid Ruy Diaz, of glorious memory and famous deeds. He returned from the province called Chile, which is far beyond the other before mentioned, called Chiriguana, and entered this great city just a year and twenty-five days after the siege had commenced.[1]

[1] Diego de Almagro was a foundling, and took his name from the town of Almagro in Castile, where he is supposed to have been born.

P

We were governed by a brother of the Governor, named Hernando Pizarro, who is a bad Christian, with no fear of God, and less devotion for our King; but pride took the place in his heart of the love of God and the King. He desired to kill me without any cause, except that he had let loose his own tongue, for he is a great and boastful talker against the King and his council. As I was a servant of the said King, I said that he should not take 100,000 *castellanos* which he had robbed from Mango-ynga, the King of this land, and from other caciques, threatening, tormenting and burning them. This was the cause of the rebellion; and not content with this, Hernando Pizarro, if any Indian wished to make his peace, would not receive him without a certain quantity of gold and silver; thus showing that he considered the gratification of his own avarice of more importance than the service of his God and his King. For these reasons he disliked me, and he intended that I should go with the men who were to have been sent to seek succour from the Governor; so that I might have been killed. This Hernando Pizarro governed very tyrannically, although this country was neither his nor his brother's. Like a tyrant he robbed and killed, favoured injustice, and encouraged Christians to fight against each other.[1] But Almagro

He came to the New World as a soldier of fortune, and his career as the joint conqueror of Peru, in company with Francisco Pizarro, is too well known to require notice here. At this time his age was between sixty and seventy; and he was returning from his expedition to Chile, one of the most wonderful and daring enterprises in the history of Spanish discovery, which is saying a great deal.

[1] Hernando Pizarro was horribly cruel, pitiless, faithless, vindictive, and avaricious, but brave as a lion, cunning, and an excellent soldier. He murdered all the Indian women he could lay his hands upon, to terrify their husbands and fathers, during the siege of Cuzco: he perjured himself and broke his word whenever it suited his purpose, as will presently be seen; and his greed for gold caused the rebellion of the Inca, and all the disasters which followed. But his bravery and reckless daring were displayed on numerous occasions; his consummate dissimulation often saved him from imminent danger, and gained him

not only had a right to come to Cuzco as a saviour, but also in obedience to the provision of the Emperor our King, which the said Hernando Pizarro had brought out with him from Spain, and which limited the jurisdiction of the Governor his brother.

Diego de Almagro, seeing that the said Hernando Pizarro was defending the place against him, and that for a great service he was giving him an evil return, remained for three or four days negotiating with us, while he and his people were covered with mud, like so many pigs. At last I wrote to him to say that I was on his side, though I feared the tyrant,[1] being tired of his pride and tyranny. Don Diego de Almagro entered the city one night, with our consent and that of the municipality, and seized the said Hernando Pizarro. The *Te Deum laudamus* was sung in the church, and we all received the said Diego de Almagro with honour and satisfaction; and for this deliverance I gave thanks to God and his blessed Mother, for if it had not come, I certainly should have had no other alternative than to join Capa-ynga, even if he had been a toad.[2]

great successes; and his skill as a general, while it crushed his brother's rival and enabled him to imbrue his hands in an old man's blood, also led him to his final retribution in the prison of Medina del Campo.

At this time he was advanced in years, a very large coarse man, with a repulsive hard countenance, bulbous red nose, and insolent manner. He was the eldest and only legitimate brother of the Pizarros.

[1] In a Royal Order of the Emperor, dated at Barcelona, March 14th, 1538, in which Almagro is condemned for his conduct, and ordered to restore Cuzco to Hernando Pizarro without delay, the following passage occurs. "The said Hernando Pizarro sent Don Alonzo Enriquez and the Licentiate Prado, who were with him in the city, to you; who, neglecting to perform the duty with which they had been entrusted, concerted with you to deliver up the city, and on another night they did deliver it up."—*Varones Illustres*, p. 223.

[2] Almagro, on his return from Chile, claimed Cuzco as part of the government granted to him by the emperor. Pizarro's province was to extend for two hundred and seventy-five leagues, and Almagro's was to commence where his rival's ended. But the point where the line was to

## XLVIII.

OF WHAT HAPPENED TO MYSELF PRINCIPALLY, ALTHOUGH I SHALL NOT
FAIL TO RELATE OTHER THINGS WHICH HAVE SOME CONNECTION
WITH MY AFFAIRS.

This Adelantado Don Diego de Almagro, Governor of
this kingdom called the kingdom of New Toledo, began to
govern, both by good acts and good intentions, for the service of God and the King, much to the satisfaction of the
people whom he found in the city, as well as of those whom
he brought with him.   He honoured and rewarded many of
his followers, not forgetting to punish those who had acted
in defiance of the King's orders.   So far as concerns myself, he embraced me, received me like a son, and, after two
days, he said to me :—" Don Alonzo, as well in consideration of your being a servant of the Emperor, as for your
own merits, I desire to treat you as you deserve; and if I
should forget to summon you to my secret councils, you

commence was not fixed, nor was it specified how it was to be measured,
and in short the question of the boundary was a very complicated and difficult one, even for an unprejudiced person to decide. But in quitting Cuzco
to conquer what he considered his province further south, Almagro had
virtually conceded the point; and he now returned to reopen the question,
after finding the bleak plains of the Collao and of Chile, and the sandy
wastes of Atacama, very distasteful both to himself and to his followers.

Almagro sent to Hernando Pizarro, claiming Cuzco as a part of his
province, and encamped within a short distance of the city.   Pizarro
demanded that Almagro should lay his powers, which he stated that he
possessed, before the city Council; and this was done, on condition that
Pizarro absented himself from the Council, a short truce being agreed
upon at the same time.   The Council decided that Almagro must not
occupy the city until the question of the boundary was settled.   On the
same night, however, the 8th of April, 1537, Almagro forced his way
into the city, and threw Hernando Pizarro into prison, on pretence that
he was fortifying his position, contrary to the terms of the truce.

This latter version is, I believe, the true one, and excuses Almagro's
apparent breach of-faith.   Don Alonzo gives an account of the transaction in two other places further on, in a letter to the emperor,
and in a paper of accusations against Hernando Pizarro.

must not on that account fail to be present, because I wish to favour and assist you on every occasion in my power."

After our Governor, the Adelantado Don Diego de Almagro, captured that most turbulent and excessively proud tyrant Hernando Pizarro; he who, as I have already stated, held both God and the King as of little account, and myself as of still less; he sent, and this is God's truth, one of his servants, named Francisco Maldonado, to me, to ask me to have pity on him, and not to act against his interests, and he also presented me with a vase of gold.

All the time that we were besieged, and afterwards, Don Francisco Pizarro, the Governor of the province called New Castile, pretended to a right over this province also, which is called New Toledo, and in the language of the Indians Cuzco; because he had discovered and conquered it. But Don Diego de Almagro also shared in the discovery and conquest; for in their labours and designs the two had been companions for a long time, and the Emperor and King our Lord, by his royal provision, had made Don Diego Governor of the province of New Toledo, which was to extend for two hundred and sixty leagues beyond the limits of New Castile.

Don Francisco Pizarro, believing that Almagro had died in his expedition, and desiring to possess all the land, as well as to succour his brothers who were besieged in this city of Cuzco, assembled a large body of horse and foot, with defensive and offensive arms. The City of the Kings, a seaport of the province of New Castile, one hundred and twenty leagues from Cuzco, was also besieged and pressed hard by the Indians; yet he dispatched five hundred men to Cuzco, led by an ignorant captain, named Alonzo de Alvarado,[1] who approached very slowly and lazily. The

---

[1] Alonzo de Alvarado, a native of Burgos, first came to Peru with his relative the famous Adelantado Pedro de Alvarado. He was wounded in the thigh in a battle with the Indians, led by Atahualpa's general

Governor, Don Diego de Almagro, sent another five hundred men to meet him at a distance of twenty-five leagues from Cuzco. A messenger was also sent to tell him that if he came to help the besieged, his assistance was no longer required; but that his services might still be useful, because the Inga, the Indian Lord of this land, had retired with a large body of natives. The messengers were Juan de Guzman, Diego de Mercado, the Licentiate Francisco de Prado, Diego and Gomez de Alvarado, and the author of this present book.[1] We travelled all night, and arrived at the camp of Alvarado at dawn, which we found in a very strong position, surrounded by lofty mountains. In front of the camp flowed a broad and rapid river, spanned by a bridge which was defended by pieces of artillery.

The said Captain Alvarado received us courteously and

Quizquiz. He afterwards invaded the province of Chachapoyas in Northern Peru, and, on his return, was sent by Pizarro with succour, to the besieged garrison at Cuzco. Thus he now found himself in a position of difficulty, but he at once determined to oppose the claims of Almagro. After his defeat at Abancay, he escaped from Almagro's prison at Cuzco, and reached Lima in company with Gonzalo Pizarro. He was with Hernando Pizarro at the battle of Las Salinas, and afterwards retired to his government of Chachapoyas. He collected troops at Huanuco and fought on the side of Vaca de Castro at the battle of Chupas. Returning to Spain, he went out again with the President Gasca, was appointed " Maestro del Campo" of his army, and was present at the battle of Xaquixaguana. Afterwards he was one of the judges to try Gonzalo Pizarro and Carbajal. He was then made Corregidor of Cuzco, and subsequently of Charcas, whither he was sent, by the Royal Audience, to crush the revolt of Sebastian de Castilla. His extreme severity enabled Francisco Hernandez Giron to organize an insurrection at Cuzco in 1553. Alvarado advanced against him, and was defeated at Chuquinga. The chagrin and mortification caused by this disaster preyed on his mind, and he died soon afterwards, in about 1556.

[1] Herrera, in mentioning this embassy, merely says, " Diego and Gomez de Alvarado, and some others." Dec. iv, lib. iv, cap. 2. Garcilasso de la Vega says, " Diego de Alvarado and eight other knights, from the most noble whom he had with him." Pte. ii, lib. ii, cap. 33. Thus neither of these historians mentions our author, Don Alonzo, by name, on this occasion.

with open arms on the bridge, and conducted us up the side of the mountain to his quarters, where there were many knights and honourable persons, and where we were invited to dinner. Afterwards he stood up in the midst of his officers, and said : " Gentlemen, I come to succour the city of Cuzco, by order of my master Don Francisco Pizarro, because it is a part of his territory, and because he believed that Don Diego de Almagro was dead. I now hear that he has entered by force into the city of Cuzco, and made the inhabitants obey him as their Governor, seizing Hernando and Gonzalo Pizarro, the brothers of our master, with the intention of beheading them ; for which reason I shall detain your worships."

We answered that Hernando and Gonzalo Pizarro were imprisoned for their crimes, and for having opposed the execution of the king's orders (which we brought with us and presented to him), but that we were messengers, and were guilty of no fault whatever. He neither looked at the orders, nor would he allow us to finish what we had to say, observing, that to settle the boundaries it would be necessary for the Emperor to send out an umpire. He then took away our swords, and put us in irons, under the charge of a strong guard. Afterwards he employed many Indians to build a stone prison, into which he put us, with guards on every side, and he would not allow us to see or speak to any of his people, lest we should enlighten them as to the justice of the cause of Don Diego de Almagro, and the treason which their Captain was committing in rebelling against the orders of the king. He also stationed two knights in the prison with us, to prevent us from writing, or speaking to the guards, and these two men never left us day or night.[1]

[1] Garcilasso de la Vega says that three honourable knights, in Alvarado's company, namely, his own father, Garcilasso de la Vega, Alvarez Holguin, and Gomez de Tordoya, protested against this treatment of ambassadors.

Mr. Helps excuses it, on the ground that Almagro had previously at-

When Don Diego de Almagro heard this, he sent an
alcalde and a secretary to require, on the part of the king,
that his messengers, who were detained in prison, should be
released, and that Alvarado should hear the royal provision
by which His Majesty had made Almagro Governor of this
land; declaring that if he refused, he would come for the
prisoners, and punish those who detained them, as traitors.
The lazy and headstrong Captain never consulted any one
excepting one Gomez de Tordoya, who was banished from
all the territories of the Emperor and King our Lord, sentenced to a hundred thousand deaths as a traitor, a lover of
strife and rebellion, an enemy of peace and justice, who was
suffered to serve by Don Francisco Pizarro, because he was
a native of his province of Estremadura.[1] Having consulted
this man, Alvarado replied that his people knew no Governor except Francisco Pizarro, and that he would neither
hear the royal provision, nor give up his prisoners. Gomez
de Tordoya added that he had had enough of the docu-
ments of the lawyers of the King's council.

Don Diego de Almagro, reflecting on the reasonable
nature of his demands and the justice of his cause, marched
out of Cuzco with four hundred and fifty men, and reached

tempted to deceive Alvarado by a forged letter; and he adds that the
envoy received much courtesy from their captor. Vol. iv, p. 72. Per-
haps it can hardly be expected that our author, who was one of the suf-
ferers, should be of the same opinion.

[1] Gomez de Tordoya came to Peru with Don Pedro de Alvarado. He was
a native of Badajos. He was a devoted friend and follower of Francisco
Pizarro, and at the time of the Governor's murder, was a member of the
municipality of Cuzco. The tidings of his friend's death reached him
when he was out hawking in the vicinity of the city; and he, turning to
his falcon, exclaimed, "Now will come a time of fire and blood, and not
of hawking and pleasure." He of course refused to join the party of
the younger Almagro, but became a captain in the army of Vaca de
Castro, and was killed fighting bravely at the bloody battle of Chupas.
He was buried in a little church at Guamanga, which is still standing.

The abuse of this knight by our author, is, so far as I can gather from
other sources, quite undeserved.

the opposite side of the river. He then sent his confessor
to say that Alvarado ought not to be the cause of the death of
so many Spaniards, to which that captain replied that he had
sent three mounted messengers to the governor to tell him
the state of affairs, which was true, and that he would
rather die with all his people than comply with a single
demand until the return of the messengers. When we
prisoners knew this, and saw the danger of Alvarado's
position, and that Don Diego de Almagro was about to
make an appeal to arms for our sakes, we sent to this headstrong captain to propose that two of us should go down to
the bridge, and say that if, for our sakes, Don Diego was
about to fight, he should not do so. The said captain consented, and said that we must arrange amongst ourselves as
to the choice of two envoys. The Licentiate Prado and
myself were selected, and we went down in company with
the captain, to whom I said many things on the road.
Especially I remember saying—" Recollect, sir, that if the
brothers of your governor are unjustly imprisoned, to
release whom you have come with arms in your hands, you
are not the judge in this cause, that even if you should
conquer you will be conquered, and punished for the mischief you will have done." But he would neither listen to
my rebuke, nor to my good advice, and God paid him in
the following manner. When we arrived on the banks of
the river, the artillery began to play on both sides; and as
the engagement was commenced on the side of the Governor
Don Diego de Almagro, the said captain was greatly enraged, and ordered us to return to the prison. He began
the battle like a lion, but he ended it like a fox, taking
refuge in the mountains, with Gomez de Tordoya; while
the governor and his lieutenant Captain Rodrigo Orgoñez, a
valiant knight, enterprising and experienced in manœuvring
cavalry, remained in possession of the camp. The troops
crossed the river, the cavalry by a ford, and the infantry

Q

across the bridge; and, as God is just, and rebukes the pride of those who give him cause, it is true that, when they entered, the water did not come up to their stirrups, while when they returned many were drowned, the river being much swollen, although no rain had fallen.

The party of Alvarado surrendered, only three' or four being killed, and our deliverers came up and let us out, after we had suffered in that solitary prison for twenty-seven days. I feared all the time that they would put me to death, because I was an enemy of Hernando Pizarro; and I joyfully returned to Cuzco with the victorious party, while Alonzo de Alvarado and Gomez de Tordoya accompanied us as prisoners.[1]

[1] When I was at Abancay, in 1853, I took some pains to trace out the scene of these events, and the site of Alvarado's camp. The modern town of Abancay is situated in a very beautiful valley, through which the river flows, and is bounded on either side by steep and lofty spurs of the Andes. Abancay is a pretty little town consisting of a *plaza* with a stone church, and a few streets leading from it, and the environs are surrounded by fruit gardens and clumps of tall trees. On the south-west of the town there is a deep ravine, with its sides covered with delicious flowers, through the bottom of which runs the rapid river of Abancay, which empties itself into the Pachachaca, a tributary of the Apurimac. It was probably at this point that Almagro effected the passage of the river, his infantry crossing by a bridge, and his cavalry by a ford a little lower down.

On the opposite side a range of mountains rises abruptly from the river, to such a height, that their rocky summits are frequently covered with snow, and it is here that the varied productions of a country doubly blessed by nature may be seen at one glance. Near the summit large herds of cattle and flocks of sheep were feeding on rich pasture; lower down there were extensive patches of wheat, barley, and potatoes; then followed broad fields of maize; while on the banks of the river were sugar canes, orange and citrons trees, and all the rich fruits of the tropics.

On an isolated hill, a few hundred feet above the river, there is an ancient stone building, now almost concealed by creepers and small shrubs which cover its crumbling walls. It is called by the Indians *Huacca-pata* (the hill of mourning), and tradition connects its origin with the name of Alonzo de Alvarado. I examined it very carefully; it

I had forgotten to say that, in the encounter at the ford, the Lieutenant Rodrigo Orgoñez received a blow in the face from a stone, and fell to the ground apparently dead; but presently he got up and led his men to the height, where we were in prison.[1] After the battle an Indian chief, who was at the head of 2,000 Indians, made a speech to the governor, which seems to me to be worthy of remembrance. "Apo!"—a word which means chief in their language—"I am captain of this people, and up to the time of your arrival I have been in arms, and have killed many Christians in the cause of my Capa-ynga; for we have suffered great evils from them. You ought not, therefore, to be astonished at this, nor ought the great Apo of Castile; for before your arrival, we were lords, and now we are slaves. Not only have the Christians ceased to treat us as becomes our rank,—the nobles as nobles, the officers as officers, and the peasants as peasants,—but they have treated all alike, and they want us all to carry their burdens on our backs. Have we not reason, then, to resent this? And we ask you to remedy all the injuries which we suffer from your people."

## XLIX.

I HAVE SEEN ALL THINGS IN THE WORLD, AND FOR THIS I GIVE ALL THE PRAISE TO GOD ALONE, WHO IS SOVEREIGN LORD.

There are four seas in the world, and I have navigated them all; and though I have not been in every part of the world, yet there is little left for me to see, in this the last month of the year 1538. *Mundo* is a Latin word, in Romance

is certainly not an edifice of Inca origin, and I think it very probable that this is the very building which our author here describes as having been hastily built as a prison, for the detention of himself and his colleagues.

[1] The battle took place on the 12th of July, 1537.

it means *clean,* and so God intended it to be, and that we should go to heaven and not to hell. But I must return to the consideration of the seas, which, as I have before said, are four in number. One they call the Western sea, which washes the coasts of Biscay, Holland, and Greenland, as well as Ireland, England, and Flanders. Another is called the Eastern sea, which borders on part of France, Genoa, Calabria, Apulia, Rhodes, and Turkey. Another is the Ocean sea, washing the shores of Barbary, Santa Martha, Carthagena, and New Spain. The fourth is the South sea, along the coasts of Nigaragua, Guatemala, and New Spain. I would also have you to know that all these four seas may be said to be one, for they flow into each other, and are only divided by narrow straits.[1]

I now desire to inform you of the end of all these hostilities and differences respecting boundaries, between the two Governors. I am obliged to both of them, though more, both in quality and quantity, to Don Diego de Almagro than to the other; and I consider that the former was more devoted to the service of God and the King, than the latter. I, being a messenger from Don Diego de Almagro to Don Francisco Pizarro, going from one camp to the other, always laboured to establish peace. Thus I was selected and chosen as one out of four, to consider the settlement of these differences. On the part of Don Francisco Pizarro there were, a knight named Francisco de Chaves, an officer of cavalry and his relation, and the Friar Juan de Olias, Provincial of the Dominicans; and on the part of Don Diego de Almagro were Diego Nuñez de Mercado, Alcalde of Nicaragua for his Majesty, and myself. The settlement of the boundary between the two governments, and the arrangements for establishing peace, were entrusted to us

---

[1] This outburst of geography, on the part of Don Alonzo, is probably the result of his studies and cogitations on the boundary question between Pizarro and Almagro.

four.[1]   A friar named Francisco de Bobadilla, Provincial of
the order of our Lady of Mercy, afterwards meddled in the
affair, and passed from one camp to the other.   The devil
always seeks for suitable men to do his will in affairs of importance; and he, therefore, chose this friar, who said to
Don Diego: " I regret that you should have trusted your
honour and estate to four covetous persons, thus placing
what you have gained with so much labour in great
danger; for these four cannot arrange this affair, two of
them taking the part of their master, and the other two of
theirs.   You ought to appoint a judge between them."   Don
Diego de Almagro replied : " I know of no man, either on
my side or on the other, who is fit for such a post, unless it
be your reverence."   He answered : " If you leave the
business in my hands, I swear to you by the habit of our
Lady of Mercy which I have received, to give you the
boundary you have claimed, until a competent judge shall
have arrived from his Majesty the King our lord."   Don
Diego was so well pleased at this promise that he sent to
revoke our powers, and gave them to this friar.

The friar then stationed himself between the two camps,[2]

[1] Garcilasso de la Vega mentions our author as one of the commissioners on this occasion.   *Comm. Real.*, Pte. ii, lib. ii, cap. xxxv.   Herrera does not give the names of the commissioners. Dec. iv, lib. iv, cap. ii.
Garcilasso says that these commissioners were unable to come to any
conclusion, and that, therefore, the decision was referred to the Friar
Bobadilla, by the mutual consent of Pizarro and Almagro.

Herrera tells us that, when Almagro's commissioners were on their
way to Lima, Pizarro sent Alonzo Alvarez with thirty men to intercept
them at Mala, on the coast.   He took away their horses, mounted them
on mules, and conducted them under a guard to Lima, where Pizarro
conferred with them.   Pizarro y Orellana gives the name of Alonzo Enriquez, as one of the boundary commissioners." *Varones Illustres*, p. 178.

[2] At Mala, on the coat of Peru, fifty miles south of Lima.   Approaching from Lima, after a long ride over a sandy desert, the beautiful vale of
Mala comes suddenly in sight.   It is watered by a river of the same
name, which flows rapidly from the gorges of the Andes, and falls into
the Pacific.   On both sides, north and south, there is a desolate sandy

and ordered the two governors to appear before him, each accompanied by twelve armed knights; and I was one of those who went with Don Diego de Almagro. The friar and Don Francisco Pizarro behaved with duplicity, and concealed a large body of men to seize and kill us, if we should not agree to what they desired. It is due to the Divine goodness and to the justice of Don Diego de Almagro, that he did all that Don Francisco Pizarro wished. The question of the imprisonment of Hernando Pizarro, and many others, besides that of the boundary, were left to the friar, whom we may compare to Judas. The two governors having retired to their camps, the friar gave his sentence, despoiling Don Diego de Almagro of all his province. In consequence of this sentence, we were afterwards exposed to great dangers and hardships, for Don Diego de Almagro appealed against the deceitful sentence, and said that he would lose fifty thousand *castellanos* before he would consent to it; especially as the friar had pronounced judgment on matters over which he had been given no jurisdiction.[1]

waste; but the valley itself is covered with fields of sugar cane, vines, maize, and lucerne, while the roads are shaded by orange and fig trees, and tall willows.

[1] The Royal Provision, brought out by Hernando Pizarro, which was the cause of the dispute, enacted that Pizarro should receive, as his province, all the country extending along a meridian south from the river of Santiago for two hundred and seventy leagues, including all countries east and west within this latitude. Almagro's province was to commence where Pizarro's ended, and to extend for two hundred leagues further south.

There seems to be little doubt that Pizarro intended to have treacherously seized Almagro during the interview at Mala, and that the latter was warned of his danger by a knight named Francisco de Godoy, who sang the first words of an old song, in his hearing,—

> " Tiempo es cavallero—
> Tiempo es ya de andar de aqui."

He rode away with his knights, across the sandy desert, to Lunahuana, in the upper part of the fertile valley of Cañete, to which point his Lieutenant Orgoñez, fearing treachery, had advanced with his little army.

## L.

The hardships which must be endured in these countries
are so terrible, that the men who come to them, in order that
they may not yield up their spirits, nor lose all their flesh,
nor despair of the divine clemency, must not be over dainty,
nor, to say truth, over wise; they must be hardy and
vigorous, not made of flesh and blood, but of iron and steel.
O sinner that I am! to have come here to damage my conscience, waste my time, and lose my teeth. While one is
seeking for riches, it is necessary to pass such an infernal
life that, when they are attained, one has neither teeth to
eat with, nor stomach to digest.

Now I desire to relate the affairs of these two governors.
They had pitched their tents at a distance of about a league
from each other.[1] Don Hernando Pizarro had five hundred
cavalry and three hundred arquebusiers and crossbow men,
and he intended to occupy the place where we were encamped, which, in the Indian language, is called Huaytara.[2]
Don Diego de Almagro had three hundred cavalry and one

The Friar Bobadilla, who was evidently a mere creature of Pizarro,
and had completely deceived the less suspicious mind of Almagro, pronounced judgment on the boundary question, on November 15th, 1537.
He decided that, as the position of the starting point, Santiago itself,
was not fixed, it would be necessary to send pilots and notaries in a ship,
to settle that question ; and that in the meanwhile Almagro must surrender Cuzco to Pizarro within thirty days, and give up all his prisoners
within six ; that Pizarro should furnish his rival with a ship to take his
dispatches to the King ; that both sides should disband their armies ;
and that there should be perpetual peace between them.

[1] Don Alonzo here omits all allusion to the transactions between the
interview at Mala, and the retreat of Almagro to Huaytara ; but further
on, in a letter to the Emperor, he makes up this deficiency in his narrative.

[2] A wild pass in the Andes, above the coast valley of Pisco.

hundred infantry; but though his troops were fewer in number, they were more accustomed to the work, for they had marched together for many long and weary leagues. At this time a horse had come to be worth seven thousand *castellanos,* and the prices of other things had risen in the same proportion; yet the men were resolved to die rather than yield up the province. But they determined not to fight at a disadvantage, to the detriment of the Emperor's service, and therefore began to retreat in good order; the baggage in front, and the armed men in the rear, formed in squadrons.

Now, although the encampments were so close to each other, yet one was in summer and the other in winter; for Don Diego de Almagro was in the *sierra,* while Pizarro was below: and in the *sierra* it rains and snows for half the year, while on the coast it never rains. When the soldiers of Pizarro followed us, and came up into the cold, being unaccustomed to such a climate, and recently arrived in the country, they began to fall back. Their commander was Hernando Pizarro, who, as I have before said, was a passionate man, with little fear of either God or the king; but he yielded to necessity, and led them back to the valley of Yca.[1]

[1] Almagro, having liberated Hernando Pizarro, found himself threatened by his rivals, and, retreating up the valley of Pisco, he entrenched himself in the wild and almost inaccessible pass of Huaytara in the Cordillera which overhangs the coast valley. Hernando Pizarro, with three hundred men, scaled the heights, and Almagro commenced his retreat towards Cuzco. Had he taken this opportunity of falling upon his enemy, he would certainly have crushed him, for Pizarro's men were mostly fresh arrivals; the sudden change from the warm coast valleys to the snowy heights had brought on the *sorochi* or sickness of the Andes, and they were not at all in good fighting condition.

This *sorochi,* caused by the rarefaction of the air at great elevations, always attacks new comers. It is compared to "sea sickness," but I can say from experience that it is infinitely worse, for to excessive nausea is added violent headache and giddiness. Pizarro's men, attacked by this malady, were certainly in no condition to fight a battle. He, therefore,

I, as a servant of the King, and as a person of quality, desiring to retire with the fruits of my labours, which were 2,000 *castellanos*, had done all in my power to establish peace; and if I had served and favoured Don Diego de Almagro, it was because he had appointed me as his representative, and because he had justice on his side. I cried Peace, Peace, and wrote many letters which I do not give here, to avoid prolixity, and because I do not wish to fill up this book with letters. I cannot, however, resist putting in the following letter, because it gave me some satisfaction to write it to the Friar Francisco de Bobadilla, Father Provincial of the Order of Our Lady of Mercy; and his reply follows: and afterwards I will relate what happened next, if I do not die first.

"Very reverend and magnificent Sir,—I am suspicious that, owing to my warlike profession, your paternity, whom I desire to serve, will not believe that I am a peaceful man, zealous for the service of God and the King, and for the honour of the Governor Don Francisco Pizarro, but that you will suspect that I wish for a rupture; yet I can assure your paternity that, had it not been for me, and the Licentiate Prado, we should already have returned to Lima and Cuzco. I remember that, when his majesty the emperor sent me as his captain general of Iviça to defend the island against Barbaroja, I issued, amongst many other orders, one which was as follows :—' We also command and charge you that if the Moors, enemies of our holy Catholic faith, who are coming to attack this city and island, fall into your hands, you shall labour to capture as many as you can

led them down into the fertile valley of Yca to recruit, while his brother the Marquis Francisco Pizarro, unfit, from his advanced age, to bear the fatigues of the campaign, returned to Lima. The rich valley of Yca, forty-two miles south-east of Pisco, is a wide expanse of fertile land, at the foot of the maritime Cordillera, and surrounded on all other sides by a sandy desert. It is now covered with vineyards and cotton plantations, while its streams are bordered by tall willows.

R

alive, and to kill as few as possible.' Thus you see that I am very peaceful; but I am surprised to hear it said that your paternity is for peace; for if you are for us, who, then, is against us? How can this be when you are influenced by the passions of Don Hernando Pizarro, and the importunities of the citizens of Cuzco. I well know what the philosopher says of a man, with his own passions and interests to serve, being admitted into council, such as this Hernando Pizarro; and the people of Cuzco are covetous because they fear that their lands will be taken from them and given to the men of Chile. You should be content, without desiring to gain more, in spite of God and the King, and at the cost of so many Christian lives. May God guard the very reverend and magnificent person of your paternity, so that you may be a father in this world, and a saint in the next. Dated from this camp of Huaytara, January 1st, 1538. At the service of your paternity,

"ALONZO ENRIQUEZ DE GUZMAN."

Here follows the reply of the friar to my letter:—

" Very magnificent Sir,—May the grace of the Holy Spirit be with your worship. I received your wise letter, and am unable to answer it, seeking pardon from your worship if in anything I have offended you. Your servant, the Friar Francisco de Bobadilla, Provincial of our Lady of Mercy."

## LI.

### WHAT HAPPENED IN THE WAR BETWEEN THESE TWO GOVERNORS.

The Governor Don Francisco Pizarro left Lima and marched towards the camp at Huaytara, where was the Governor Don Diego de Almagro. He halted at a distance of eight leagues, and his brother Hernando, like a man despairing of divine clemency, led the dance. This man, at dawn, led his men up the pass; and Don Diego de Almagro, to avoid risking the cause of the Emperor and of God upon one venture, retreated. We were followed for three days by Hernando Pizarro's men, who captured some of our tents and beds; but we turned and put them to flight, taking three prisoners. We came to a province called Vilca,[1] where there is plenty of provisions, and where we were nearer to Cuzco; while Pizarro's army retired to the valley of Yca, six days journey from our position, to recruit his strength.

In travelling over these rugged and lofty mountains, on a horse which was worth 2,000 ducats, we both fell down a precipice, for a distance of a sling's throw, without any lies. The horse was dashed to pieces, and I broke my left arm, bruised my leg, and received a wound on my head. I remained in such a state that, though those who found me heard me say "Credo in Deum," yet, when they had carried me three leagues in an Indian hammock, to a place called ,[2] I did not know what had happened. You now see how fortunes are gained out here; and I declare, on my faith, that, if they offered to make me a king on condition that I went through all this again, I would not do it, but that I would rather be a doctor's stirrup boy.

I also lost my bed, provisions, store of gold and silver, and clothes. I have now been two years, against my will, in this country of Indians, and here I am now in the city of Cuzco, detained by the civil wars and disputes of these two governors, without caring more for the one than for the other. I swear by God, and on this cross, ✠, that if I was asked which of the two I desired to be victorious in the dispute, I should say the one who has justice on his side.

I remained very ill for a long time, without knowing

---

[1] In the *sierra*, not far from the modern city of Ayacucho.
[2] Illegible in MS.

whether I had any left arm or not; and, for want of medicines, I was cured with bandages of cotton kept damp, with canes for splints.

Don Diego de Almagro retreated, and placed many rivers and mountains between himself and his enemy, because Pizarro's followers were nearly double his own in number. Our forces retreated, and wintered in a province called Vilca, whence Don Diego sent to the great city of Cuzco, where he had stationed a very honourable knight, named Diego de Alvarado,[1] as his lieutenant and captain general, with four hundred men, ordering him to come to Vilca in person with two hundred men, a distance of forty leagues. This would increase Almagro's force to six hundred men. He also sent me to the city of Cuzco, to act as his captain general.   Soon after the arrival of the said Alvarado at Vilca, the Governor Don Diego de Almagro fell so ill that we thought he was dying, and there was great sorrow in the camp; for the people not only loved him for his liberal disposition, but also feared that his death would be a great loss to them.   When he thought that his last moments were come, he said—" My death does not afflict me, for I am an old man; but I am grieved because I must leave so many brave knights and dear companions and friends who have fought for me, without any provision.   I would, therefore, only seek from God sufficient time to accomplish the enter- prize I have on hand."

[1] Diego de Alvarado was a brother of the famous Pedro de Alvarado, who took so prominent a part in the conquest of Mexico under Cortes. He came to Peru with his brother, and became a follower of Almagro, with whom he continued until that chief's death.  He was a noble minded, honourable, and merciful knight, and it would have been well for Almagro if he had always followed the advice of so good a councillor. On the death of Almagro, Diego de Alvarado immediately returned to Spain, to plead the cause of the younger Almagro, and demand justice on Hernando Pizarro.  He challenged his adversary to single combat, but died five days after he had sent the challenge, not without suspicion of poison.

On account of my fall and the breaking of my arm, he gave me at the same time 2,000 *castellanos*; and, as he had not sufficient gold, he ordered a paper to be delivered to me, signed by his mayor-domo, on the 13th of February, 1538, in which he acknowledged the debt, for he himself could not write, and his mayor-domo signed for him. I now desire to explain how well I deserved this present. First, I had risked my life three times for this governor, and on another occasion I had been imprisoned and ill-treated for his sake; second, I had fallen down and broken my arm; third, I had passed through many privations and hardships in his service; fourth, the enemy had killed a negress of mine, who had cost me six hundred *castellanos*; and lastly, I had lost my clothes, the bed in which I slept, my provisions, and my store of gold and silver, worth altogether 2,000 *castellanos*.

My appointment as captain general of Cuzco was signed in the province of Vilca, in New Toledo, on the 10th of February, 1538.

## LII.

HOW THE GOVERNOR SALLIED FORTH FROM THE CITY OF CUZCO, TO DEFEND IT AGAINST THE FURY AND TYRANNY OF THOSE WHO SOUGHT TO USURP HIS GOVERNMENT.

The said governor, Don Diego de Almagro, though he was determined to come out and defend the city of Cuzco against Hernando Pizarro and his followers, yet, to make his cause more just, he resolved not to march forth until it was absolutely necessary.[1] Thus it was that the said Hernando Pizarro arrived within a short distance with eight hundred men; four hundred cavalry, one hundred and thirty arquebusiers, and the rest crossbow men.[2] The go-

[1] Almagro arrived at Cuzco a month earlier than Hernando Pizarro.

[2] He had marched from his quarters at Yca to the green vale of Nasca on the coast, and then over the cordilleras by Lucanas, to Cuzco.

vernor at last sallied out, and slept at a distance of half a
league from the city, with six hundred men, three hundred
of them cavalry, commanded by his captain general, Rodrigo
Orgoñez.   I do not desire to begin praising this knight, lest
I should never end, but he gave proof of his qualities in the
Italian wars.[1]

It was on a Saturday that the two armies encountered
each other ;[2] and, as the governor was very ill, he entrusted
the command to his lieutenant Orgoñez, while he remained
a sling's throw in the rear, with some friars.

The battle then began ;[3] and the captain general Rodrigo
Orgoñez said to one of his captains, who commanded fifty
men, seeing that the arquebusiers of the enemy were galling
his troops,—" Charge, sir, with your squadron, and disperse
me those arquebusiers."   He answered (I do not put his
name, for the sake of his honour)[4] " Would you send me to
be butchered ?"   Then the said Rodrigo Orgoñez raised his
eyes to heaven, exclaiming, " Shield me, Almighty God !"

---

[1] Rodrigo de Orgoñez was a fierce soldier, who always advised extreme
measures, and was the very opposite of Diego de Alvarado, Almagro's
other principal commander and adviser.   He had served under the Constable of Bourbon at the sack of Rome ; and, after his arrival in Peru,
continued true to the fortunes of Almagro, until his death on the bloody
field of Las Salinas.

[2] April 26th, 1538 ; or, according to our author, who here agrees with
Garcilasso de la Vega, April 6th, the day after the feast of St. Lazarus.

[3] This was the battle of Las Salinas, which decided the fate of
Almagro.

[4] The cavalry of Almagro's army, under Orgoñez, was in four divi-
sions, commanded by Juan Tello, Vasco de Guevara, Francisco de Chaves,
and Ruy Diaz Orgoñez.   Tello was beheaded at Guamanga, after the
battle of Chupas, where he had fought for the younger Almagro.   The
last we hear of Guevara was that he fled from the interior to Lima, when
Giron's rebellion broke out in 1553.   Chaves served as a captain under
Almagro the younger.   Ruy Diaz Orgoñez was murdered by Pizarro's
soldiers, after he had surrendered.   At this distance of time we cannot
tell which of these four knights failed in his duty on this occasion, nor
is there any reason why our author's desire to screen the name of the
delinquent should not be respected.

and attacked the enemy single handed, mounted on a light
grey horse. He speared a foot soldier, cut open the head of
an arquebusier, and wounded another in the thigh, returning
to the ranks of his own men, in the face of the enemy, who
were waiting an attack like men of war, as in truth Hernando Pizarro really was, and then proved himself to be.
But the enemy made great havoc from a distance with their
arquebuses, and when the captain Rodrigo Orgoñez saw
this, being enraged at the misconduct of the bad captain, he
cried out to his followers, " Santiago !" and, followed by no
more than a hundred worthy and valiant men, charged the
enemy, and fell in the first encounter. There fell with him
the captain Pedro de Lerma, a Portuguese named Nicolas
de Lemos, a knight of Xeres named Diego de Vera, another
knight named Hernando de Alvarado, and Gregorio Enriquez de Herrera. The rest of Almagro's troops were soon
dispersed, though not without the loss of about twenty on
the other side.[1]

[1] The battle which decided the fate of Almagro and his party was
fought at a place called " Las Salinas," or the salt pits, about a league
from Cuzco. Almagro's army was superior in cavalry, but the Pizarros
had an immense advantage in firearms, and in the discipline of the
veterans who wielded them. A new kind of bullet, recently invented in
Flanders, was used by Pizarro's party in this battle, which doubtless
created as much sensation amongst military men in the sixteenth century, as the minié bullet has in our day. This bullet was formed of two
parts connected by a small chain. The links of the chain and a thin
layer of copper were first placed in the mould, so as to divide it into two
parts, and afterwards the molten lead was poured in ; which attached
itself to the ends of the chain, while the parts of the bullet were kept
separate by the copper sheet. When fired, the parts of the bullet spread
themselves to the ends of the chain, and cut all before them. With
these formidable missiles, which were brought from Flanders to Peru
by one Pedro de Vergara, the troops of the Pizarros did great execution,
and they are especially reported to have cut asunder the pikes of Almagro's soldiers. This superiority in firearms decided the day in favour of
the Pizarros, and the last gallant cavalry charge of Orgoñez, which cost
the life of that gallant soldier, and many others, failed to retrieve the
waning fortunes of Almagro. Many desperate hand to hand conflicts

Hernando Pizarro followed up his victory to the city, a distance of about a league, and upwards of two hundred fugitives were killed on the road. When the said Governor Don Diego de Almagro saw that his people were routed, he mounted a horse and fled to the city, where he found me in the *plaza*. This was the first that I heard of it, and I asked him how it was that he came thus. He replied that he came a defeated man. Presently a trumpeter arrived, and said, weeping the while, " I saw the Captain Orgoñez killed in this manner. He wanted to make his way out of the battle to recover strength, but his horse was too much exhausted, and eight or ten men fell upon him and stabbed him cruelly many times. Then he gave one of them a great blow in the neck, and cried out with a loud voice, ' By the Almighty God you shall not live to boast of this victory !' Presently he fell, and they cut off the head of this brave knight."

I then told the said governor to go up to the fortress, which overhangs the town, and proposed that we should remain there until some captain arrived. He assented to this, and went up with two or three priests and friars, afterwards surrendering to Felipe Gutierrez[1] and Gonzalo Pizarro, who secured him with fetters. I went to my lodging with five or six men, where they arrested me, and placed a guard over me, of five arquebusiers.

took place, and amongst them Pedro de Lerma and Hernando Pizarro were personally engaged, the former receiving a spear wound in the thigh, and the latter being dismounted. Finally Gonzalo Pizarro, with the infantry, charged the infantry of Almagro, and, after a brief struggle, drove them in confusion from the field. Thousands of Indians witnessed the conflict from the neighbouring hills, and naturally rejoiced to see their cruel conquerors slaughtering each other.

[1] This knight was a native of Madrid, and son of Alonzo Gutierrez, the king's treasurer. When peace was re-established in Peru, after the death of the younger Almagro, this Felipe Gutierrez was sent on an expedition of discovery to the vast forest covered country of the Moxos, to the eastward of the Andes. He was beheaded at Guamanga by order of Gonzalo Pizarro, when that chief was marching on Lima, in 1543.

At eleven o'clock at night the said five arquebusiers took me out of the city, with their matches lighted, and their arquebuses on their shoulders. They then ordered me to salute them; so I took off my cap and said, " I kiss the hands of your worships." They then said that they had heard that I was rich, and that I had twenty-five thousand *castellanos*; and I replied that the noise about it was more than the money. They then tied my hands behind my back, and drew the cords very tight; so I said, " Gentlemen, how much do you desire that I should give you?" and they answered, " Five thousand *castellanos*, one thousand to each." I said, " You ask for more than I have got." One of them then said to the others, in order to frighten me, in which he succeeded, " Let us do what Hernando Pizarro ordered us to do." I then felt certain that they intended to kill me, judging from the cruelties which Hernando Pizarro had perpetrated on that day; so I resolved to die, and not to give them a *maravedi*, for I believed that the money would not save my life, and that thus I should lose both life and money, when I wanted the latter for my wife and relations. I said, " Do what you have to do, for I will not give you a single *maravedi*," and I raised my eyes to heaven, and commended my soul to God. One of the men then put the mouth of his arquebus against my heart and fired it, but as it was not loaded it only frightened me. Another then said that as that arquebus had not gone off well, he would try his; but the same happened again, which I attributed to a miracle. They then asked me again if I would give them anything, and when I replied I had nothing there, they proposed to go with me to my lodging, where I promised to satisfy them. I there found a great friend of mine named Captain Gabriel de Rojas,[1] and I agreed to give the arquebusiers fifty *castellanos*.

[1] Garcilasso de la Vega mentions Gabriel de Rojas, together with our author, as amongst the bravest knights at the siege of Cuzco. He

On the following day I saw Hernando Pizarro, and said to him—" Sir, I trust you do not desire to take any further vengeance on me, beyond what happened last night." He replied that he pardoned me; but it is true that two months afterwards, when I was sitting one night with a great friend of mine, named Felipe Gutierrez, governor of Veragua, five armed men entered to kill me, and put their hands on their swords, and we did the same. Then we hacked at each other for the space of half-an-hour, until we were disarmed, and they left us wounded on the floor. Felipe Gutierrez had a deep cut in one hand, and smaller wounds on the head, arm, and leg; and I had so many that they were almost sufficient to kill me. I believe that Hernando Pizarro did not order this to be done, but I am sure that the men did it, believing that it would please him.

The governor was a prisoner from the day of the battle until Monday, the 8th of July, 1538, when the unfortunate man was put to death in the manner which I shall now relate.[1]

assisted Gonzalo Pizarro to escape from the prison where he was confined by Almagro, and accompanied him to Lima. He afterwards served in the army of the President Gasca, who sent him to Charcas as treasurer, where he died.

[1] Pizarro y Orellana says, "Alonzo Enriquez informed Hernando Pizarro, that there were two hundred men in the city who had conspired to rescue the Adelantado, and that they had not executed their design for want of leaders, their captains being in the power of Hernando Pizarro. He also stated that they had men stationed in a narrow pass, on the road to Los Reyes, to rescue him, if he should be sent prisoner to Spain."—*Varones Illustres del Nuevo Mundo*, p. 325. (Ed. Madrid, 1639.)

According to this account our author appears not only to have been mixed up in attempts to rescue Almagro before his execution; but to have turned traitor, and given information to Pizarro, which frustrated the plans of the conspirators. The story, however, is grossly improbable. Don Alonzo was vain, vacillating, and selfish; but he is not likely to have been guilty of such a gratuitous piece of villainy and ingratitude. See also *Spanish Conquest in America*, iv, p. 110, where Mr. Helps quotes this passage from the *Varones Illustres*.

## LIII.

THE DEATH OF THE GOVERNOR DON DIEGO DE ALMAGRO.

Hernando Pizarro instituted a process against the Governor Don Diego de Almagro, and he pleaded many things in his defence and justification, urging that the witnesses against him, as well as the judge, were influenced by malice; that some of the witnesses spoke against him in hopes of rewards from Hernando Pizarro; and others, being citizens of Cuzco, because they feared that if he escaped, their Indians might be taken from them, and given to the men of Chile. He also alleged that Hernando Pizarro could not be his judge, because he was merely the lieutenant of the governor his brother, and could not, therefore, try one who was himself a governor and adelantado; in addition to which the said Hernando was his personal enemy, whom he had detained in prison.

Notwithstanding all this, the said Hernando Pizarro one Monday morning, having assembled a great body of men in his house, entered the prison of the Adelantado and Governor Don Diego de Almagro. We may fitly call him a prince, whether we consider his honourable disposition, or the great and rich lands and lordships of this city of Cuzco, which he governed. In company with the Governor Don Francisco Pizarro he had discovered, conquered, and settled this rich land, in his own person and at his own expense. Hernando Pizarro notified the sentence of death to him; and the unfortunate old man, when he had heard it, considered it to be an abominable deed, contrary to law, justice, and reason. He was horrified, and said that he appealed to the Emperor and King Don Carlos, his lord. Hernando Pizarro answered that he should dispose his mind to think of spiritual things, for that the sentence would be executed. Then the poor old man went down on his knees on the ground, and said—"O my

Lord Don Hernando Pizarro, content yourself with the vengeance you have already enjoyed. Think that, besides the treason to God and the Emperor that my death will make you guilty of, you give me an evil return for what I have done for you ; for I was the first step of the ladder by which you and your brother rose to power.[1] Remember, too, that when you were my prisoner, those of my council importuned me to cut off your head, and I resisted, and gave you your life."

Hernando Pizarro then answered—"Sir, do not thus degrade yourself; die as bravely as you have lived; your present conduct is not that of a knight."[2] The unfortunate old man replied that he was human, and dreaded death, "although," he added, "I do not fear it so much for myself, for I am old and infirm, and have few years to live in the course of nature, but rather for the sake of so many noble knights who are my followers, and who will be lost and without a leader when I am gone." Hernando Pizarro went away, saying that he would send a friar to whom the old man might confess his sins. Then Don Diego de Almagro confessed, and made his will, leaving the Emperor all his property, and declaring that he possessed a million of dollars in gold and silver, gems and pearls, flocks and herds. To Don Diego de Almagro, a youth of eighteen years of age, his natural son, whom he dearly loved, having begotten him on an Indian girl, he left 13,500 *castellanos*; and to a daughter, named Dona Isabella de Almagro, he left 1,000 *castellanos*, desiring that she should become a nun ; and he made many other bequests to his followers and servants, and to monasteries. He named as his executors Don Diego de Alvarado,[3] Juan de Guzman, his majesty's accountant, Doctor Sepulveda,

---

[1] " Que mirase como el avia sido la mayor parte, para subir Francisco Pizarro, su caro hermano, a la cumbre de la honra que tenia."—*G. de la Vega.*   Pte. ii, lib. ii, cap. 39.

[2] Almost the same words are recorded by G. de la Vega, as having been used by Hernando Pizarro on this occasion."

[3] See note at page 124.

Juan de Herrada,[1] his mayor-domo, Juan Balsa,[2] and myself, the author of this book.

When Don Diego de Almagro had made his confession, the alguazil-mayor entered his cell, accompanied by the crier and the executioner. The governor then said : " Bear witness that this land is not for the King, for you desire to kill me, after having done his Majesty so many services. Remember that if you now think that his Majesty is far away, you will some day find that his power is near ; and even if you forget that there is a King, you cannot deny that there is a God on high who forgets nothing." The alguazil-mayor, who was named Antonio de Toraco, replied that he must die, and that nothing would avail him.

The poor old man then asked them to recall Hernando Pizarro, saying that he desired to confer with him again ; and accordingly they sent for him. The unfortunate governor said to him: " Sir, now that you are determined to kill my body, do not also destroy my soul, and your own honour. Remember that you are my enemy ; and, unless God miraculously supports me, I cannot now die with patience. If, then, you are satisfied that I deserve to die, send me to be judged by my King, the Emperor, or even by the governor your brother. If you fear that the prolongation of my life will cause trouble and confusion, I will give you any security that you may require ; and especially remember that my people are dispersed, that my lieutenant Rodrigo Orgoñez with other officers was killed in the battle, and that those who survive are in your power."

Hernando Pizarro answered that he must die, and then left him. The alguazil-major hurried the priests away, and prepared to cause the governor to be strangled in prison.

---

[1] Or de Rada.  This was the assassin of Francisco Pizarro.

[2] This knight married an Inca princess.  He joined the cause of the younger Almagro, and was killed by the Indians in the flight, after the bloody battle of Chupas in 1542.

He ordered the executioner to do what he had to do, but the executioner demurred, and said that he could not kill a prince like Don Diego de Almagro. He was, however, obliged to do it; and when he was putting the rope round his neck, the governor began to cry out with a loud voice, saying that tyrants were killing him without cause. When the deed was done, they carried the body to the *plaza* of the city, and placed it beside the gibbet, where it remained for two hours, and was afterwards interred in the monastery of our Lady of Mercy.

At this time the said Hernando Pizarro and I had become friends, because he was alive and the governor was dead, and it is very disastrous to have any intercourse with the dead.

----

## LIV.

I RETURN TO SPAIN, WHERE I AM IMPRISONED BY THE ROYAL COUNCIL
OF THE INDIES : AND HOW I RECEIVE FAVOURS FROM PRINCE
PHILIP, OUR LORD.

I must now tell you that I considered that some recompense as well of honours as of riches ought to be mixed with the anxieties, hardships, dangers, and hard work which I had gone through. That cruel tyrant, Hernando Pizarro, had also robbed me of 22,000 *castellanos,* and when I arrived in Spain, being of good birth and having many relations, and he having few, I began to complain of the robberies he had committed. I also felt it to be my duty to write a letter, both as a Christian and as a knight, relating all that I had seen in Peru.

The good Adelantado Don Diego de Almagro, was generous, frank, and liberal, loving and fearing God and the King, for whom he died.[1]    Having left me as one of the executors

[1] Mr. Prescott thus sums up the character of Almagro.  " He had
many excellent qualities by nature; and his defects, which were not few,

of his will, I looked upon myself as his messenger and representative to his Majesty, and I determined to declare the
tyrannical and foul deeds of Hernando Pizarro, and the
innocence and loyalty of the said Adelantado Don Diego de
Almagro, as you will presently see ; but I must relate how
I was received at court.

I arrived in the town of Madrid on Sunday, the 26th of
June, 1540,[1] and on Monday I went to present myself to
his Majesty, and to deliver to him the letter which I had
written, and which you will find below.    The Marquis del
Valle and Hernando Arias de Saavedra, heir to the Count
of Castellar, accompanied me ;  and we went to present ourselves to the Cardinal Archbishop of Toledo, President of
the Royal Council of the Indies, and to the Judges of the
Royal Audience.    The Emperor himself was absent in
Flanders, and the Cardinal of Toledo, with the commander
of Leon, Don Francisco de los Cobos, and others of the
Royal Council, were left to govern the kingdom.

Without seeing or hearing me, the Council of the Indies

---

may reasonably be palliated by the circumstances of his situation.    For
what extenuation is not authorized by the position of a *foundling*—
without parents, or early friends, or teachers to direct him—his little
bark set adrift on the ocean of life, to take its chance among the rude
billows and breakers, without one friendly hand stretched forth to steer
or save it !   The name of ' foundling' comprehends an apology for much,
very much that is wrong in after life."—II, p. 118.

Mr. Helps, in speaking of Almagro, says, " Profusely and splendidly
generous, he had the art of attaching men to him, who were far greater
than himself in most things ; and these attachments did not die out at
his death.    As men are seldom really attracted to other men, but by
some great quality, Almagro's generosity must have been of that deep
nature which goes far beyond gifts, and where the recipient perceives
that his benefactor loves as well as benefits him."—IV, p. 115.

[1] Don Alonzo gives no account of himself whatever between the time
of Almagro's death in July 1538, when he was at Cuzco, and June 1540,
when he turns up at Madrid.    It is to be supposed that, like Diego de
Alvarado, he set out for Spain immediately after the execution of his
unfortunate commander.

ordered me to be lodged in the house of an alguazil of the court, on pain of a fine of 10,000 ducats; for persons had arrived before me, telling lies, and closing the ears of the Emperor and of his Council against me.   As soon as my much loved lady, the most illustrious Dona Maria de Mendoza, knew of my arrest, she sent me presents, consisting of six trouts on two silver plates, and a cake upon another plate, with a message that I was not to despond, for that she would obtain justice for me.   She got permission for me to be removed to a house near her own, and sent me many and very delicate viands; and afterwards her husband Don Francisco de los Cobos came to see me.   I ought to have told you that the following letter was the cause of my return to Spain :—

"The King.

"Don Alonzo Enriquez de Guzman, it is necessary for my service that you should presently return to Spain by the first ship that sails; and if you do not come back at once, you are to be brought as a prisoner.   Barcelona, April 25th, 1538.   By order of his Majesty."

As soon as I arrived I presented myself before the Royal Council of the Indies;  and, being under arrest, I wrote to the Emperor, who, at that time, was in his county of Flanders, as follows :—

"Most puissant Lord,

"I returned from Peru in obedience to the order of your Majesty, and, on my arrival, I was put under arrest by your Royal Council of the Indies.   I now seek for justice at your hands, and I beseech you, and if it be necessary I require you, in the name of God, who is the Judge of all, to order your Council to judge me and give sentence without any long delay.   For the Pizarros,—who killed your Adelantado Don Diego de Almagro, heaping calumnies on the memory of this your good servant, whom they murdered in order to despoil him of his government, and from envy, have now informed against me—are endeavouring to take away my credit in the eyes of your Majesty. Written from Madrid, by your Majesty's humble vassal and loyal servant, who kisses your sacred hands and feet,

"DON ALONZO ENRIQUEZ DE GUZMAN."

With this letter I sent a long, complete, and true narrative of my proceedings to his Majesty; but those of the Royal Council of the Indies who were my enemies did not sleep. The rapacious old rascal of a fiscal, whose name was the Licentiate Villalobos, was one of those who sought for accusations against me. I was a prisoner for seven months; but, as God is just, and the Emperor is Catholic, I was at length released.

All this happened because the Emperor had received false information about me, and had ordered me to be seized, so that they would not release me without first consulting with his Majesty.

At this time the Prince Philip, eldest son of the Emperor and King of Spain, was fourteen years of age, very handsome in the face, though of short stature, very wise, learned, and affable, and exceedingly grave, like an Emperor and a grown man. This prince, owing to accounts given to him by friends of mine who were about his person, desired that I should be set at liberty. As soon as I was free, I went to kiss his royal hand, and was very well received. The Prince persevered in his good opinion of me; so that, if it had not been for the desire I felt to see my wife, I never would have left him, for I believe that God gave him to us for his glory.

Here follows the letter which I wrote to the Council of the Indies :—

" Most magnificent Lords,

" I beseech one and all of you to read and consider this letter. I have to say that I have not been visited by

T

my judges, although I am detained here contrary to justice
and reason; and I believe that I am imprisoned in order that
it may not be necessary to pay me, except with ingratitude ;
for such is the remedy of those who owe much, as the
Emperor our Lord does to me.   I have performed many
important services for God and the King ; for I was captain
of Germans in the siege of Tournay, and captain of five
hundred men when I succoured Don Miguel de Urrea,
Viceroy of Majorca, and recovered the island when the inhabitants were in arms against their King ; and with the
same number of men I was, for thirteen months, defending
the island of Iviça against the Moors and Frenchmen.   I
also served on the island of Los Gelves against the Moors,
and did good service in the land of Peru, as a knight and a
Christian, fighting for the faith of Jesus Christ.   Surely,
sirs, considering all this, you ought to restore me to my
honourable position, while those who so falsely deceive his
Majesty, and damage me, should be punished.   Remember,
that St. Jerome was also a prisoner, and that witnesses
against him were numerous.   O sirs, do me justice; you do
not feel what I suffer through injustice, and without having
committed any crime.   I feel for the sorrows of my mother,
who is now eighty years of age, and who writes to me to say
that she will come to me to share my prison.   I feel for the
grief of my wife, who writes to say that she had hoped that
our troubles were at an end, and that now they are commencing afresh.   I feel for the disappointment of my
brothers, friends, and relations.   Above all, I feel for my
own misfortunes.   Justice, sirs, justice.   Forget not that you
must some day be judged by one who is mightier than the
Emperor.

" Don Alonzo Enriquez de Guzman."

Soon afterwards, a decree was delivered to me from the
President and Judges of the Royal Council of the Indies, as
follows :—" Having seen the process against Don Alonzo

Enriquez de Guzman, we find that the Fiscal has not proved the things of which he is accused, and we therefore order him to be released, both in his person and his goods, until the Fiscal shall have proved the accusations which have been brought against him."

I, however, had to give securities before my person and estate were set at liberty, but the evil was that they forgot the expense and damage to which they had subjected an innocent man.

I have already told you of the favour with which Prince Philip received me. He assisted me out of pure compassion for the evils which the Emperor, his father, had brought upon me, owing to the false reports which had reached him. All the household of the prince were my friends, namely, the commander of Castile of the order of Santiago, Don Juan de Zuñiga, his mayordomo, to whom his royal person had been entrusted by the Emperor his father; Don Alonzo de Cordova, his master of the horse; and Don Pedro de Cordova, master of the household, both sons of the Count of Cabra; Don Antonio de Rojas, gentleman of the bedchamber; Don Juan de Benavides, his carver; and, finally, the Bishop of Carthagena, his tutor. Though all these gentlemen gave me their friendship, yet the chief commander of Leon, Don Francisco de los Cobos, and Dona Maria de Mendoza, his wife, were my best friends. He is a knight of noble family, of the order of Santiago. I was also indebted to the commander Juan de Serrano, his Majesty's secretary in the Royal Council of the Indies, who assisted me both by word and deed, and defended me against the vile accusations of the Fiscal.

The prince, in addition to other favours, gave me two pairs of gloves, which the Lady Infanta, who was then at Ocaña, had sent him; adding many kind and loving words, among which were these : " Don Alonzo, I would give you more, if I was able."

## LV.

I ARRIVE AT SEVILLE, MY NATIVE TOWN, AND REST THERE FOR ONE
  YEAR, RESTORING MY HEALTH AND MY FORTUNE. HOW THE ILLUS-
  TRIOUS DUKES OF MEDINA SIDONIA AND BEJAR MARRY THEIR SON
  AND DAUGHTER.

I arrived in the city of Seville, where I found my friends
and relations mourning on account of the heavy imprisonment which I had suffered, and very apprehensive concerning my health, honour, and estate.    When they at last
beheld me, eating plentifully, talking, and laughing, we all
rejoiced together.

At this time a marriage took place between Don Juan
Claros Perez de Guzman, Count of Niebla, the eldest son of
the Duke of Medina Sidonia,[1] with the Countess his wife,
daughter of the Duke of Bejar.    The Duke of Bejar, after
he had been Count of Benalcaçar, inherited the said dukedom.[2]    He was called Don Francisco de Sotomayor because
he inherited by a direct line from his father; and Zuñiga
because that is the family name of the dukedom of Bejar,
marquisate of Ayamonte, and county of Gibraleon, all which
he inherited by right of his marriage with Dona Teresa de
Zuñiga.  These were father and mother of the said Countess
of Niebla.  In the city of Seville there were great festivities
at the time of the marriage, and all the knights and ladies of
the city were invited to a feast. The Duke of Medina Sidonia
danced with the Duchess of Bejar, and the bridegroom with
the bride; and for several other days the guests danced in
the palace of the Duke of Bejar.    After fifteen days, they
conducted the bride to the palace of the Duke of Medina
Sidonia, mounted on a mule, with velvet trappings fringed
with gold.  She wore a cloak of cloth of gold, with a shirt

[1] See page 2.
[2] See pages 50 and 51, where he is mentioned as Marquis of Ayamonte, the former Duke of Bejar, his wife's uncle, being still alive.

of the same, and was escorted by many knights. The Duchess of Bejar was by her side, richly dressed, and the Duke was carried in a chair, being lame of one foot, and unable to ride. Then followed ten ladies of Seville, mounted on mules richly caparisoned, and in this order they entered the gates of the palace of the Duke of Medina Sidonia. After they had entered, the drums and trumpets were sounded within the court, for the duke would not have them sounded outside, because of the troubles between the Emperor and the King of France, allied with the Grand Turk, the enemy of our holy Catholic faith.

Crossing the courtyard, they ascended to a spacious hall, hung with cloth of gold, with a beautiful canopy of rich silk, embroidered with the arms of the Guzmans. Here there were three minstrels richly dressed, with their guitars, singing love songs; and in the same hall the Duchess of Medina Sidonia was waiting, with thirty ladies. The supper was spread in an adjoining corridor, and each course was brought in, heralded by an usher, two macebearers with silver maces, and a king-at-arms with a tabard, on which were embroidered the royal arms on one side, and the arms of the Guzmans on the other. The ladies supped on one side, and the gentlemen on the other, seventy in all; while six or seven titled persons supped in another room. After supper, the gallants danced with the ladies. This happened in November, 1541. At these feasts I dressed myself as well as I was able, in silk and brocades; and afterwards I returned to my mourning for my brother Don Luis de Guzman,[1] who had died six months before.

Afterwards I set out for the court, because the Emperor had returned to Castile from the kingdom of Aragon.

[1] See note at page 6.

## LVI.

" I do not come in person to kiss the hands of your Majesty, because I have arrived from strange lands, worn out in passing over many seas, and through wars in Peru, both with natives and Spaniards. During my absence I have done good service to your Majesty; with which I am well satisfied, and give thanks to God. If I am charged with any crime, I can defend myself by bringing forward many trustworthy witnesses, and principally by appealing to truth, and to my great services. I bring with me a broken arm, for I fell down a lofty precipice; my horse was dashed to pieces, and I only escaped by a miracle.

" In this letter, I propose, most puissant lord, to give an account of all that has befallen me, commencing with my departure, and concluding with my return; and I assure you that I set out more to advance your service, than for any object of my own. I sailed from Seville, and, in order to go to Peru, it was necessary to touch at the island of Española. I remained there for three months, because the royal audience appointed me captain-general of Santa Martha; but when certain news arrived that the adelantado of the Canaries, Don Pedro de Lugo, was on his way with a large force, I was excused.[1] From Española, most puissant lord, I went to Peru, and found the governor, Don Francisco Pizarro, in the City of the Kings. Soon afterwards, the captain Hernando Pizarro, his brother, arrived from Spain; and I went with him to the city of Cuzco, which is amongst the mountains in the interior. Cuzco is the principal city of these Indians, as Rome is amongst Christians, as well in regard of riches, as of warlike men. Here the ynga, or lord of the land resides, as well as another lord, called Villoma,[2] who is

---

[1] See page 86.                    [2] Huillac Umu.

their high priest. Here, too, is the House of the Sun, which is to them what St. Peter's at Rome is to us ; and in the surrounding mountains there are many cells, which they call *huacas*.[1] The city consists of very good houses and fine edifices ; and all the principal caciques have houses in the town, where they come to reside.

" Hernando Pizarro came as lieutenant of the governor; and after he had been there two months the ynga and villoma rebelled, with all their people, and besieged us in the city, with, I believe, as many as 200,000 men. They surrounded us so closely for the space of a year, that we gave up all hopes of escaping, as we only numbered two hundred men within the city, of whom fifty were sick, so that we only had one hundred and fifty men in fighting condition.[2]

" At the end of a year, a little more or less, the Governor Don Diego de Almagro arrived at the city with the followers whom he had brought with him from Chile. Before coming to the city, he encamped at a place called Urcos, seven leagues distant, to have an interview with the ynga and villoma, who were at a place called Tambo, also seven leagues from Cuzco. He sent two men, whom the ynga received very well ; but when he sent two more, the ynga

[1] These *huacas* are the burial places of the ancient Peruvians. The bodies were placed in a sitting posture in niches on exposed ridges of the Andes, and allowed to dry into mummies. At a place called *Huaccan-huaycu* (the vale of mourning), near Cuzco, the scarped faces of the mountains on either side of a deep gorge are literally honey-combed with thousands of these *huacas*. The same is the case near Urubamba, at a place called *Tantana-marca*.

[2] " The Inca with all his power came against Cuzco, and besieged it for eight months. Every full moon the Indians assaulted the city, which was bravely defended by Hernando Pizarro, his brothers, and many other knights and captains ; especially Gabriel de Rojas, Hernando Ponce de Leon, DON ALONZO ENRIQUES, and the treasurer Riquelme. They dared not lay aside their arms either by day or night, as men who believed for certain that the governor and all the other Spaniards were killed by the Indians."—*G. de la Vega.* Pte. ii, lib. ii, cap. 24 : quoting from *Zarate.*

detained them, saying that they wished to deceive him. Almagro then went on to Cuzco; and when Hernando Pizarro heard that he was approaching, without having sent any previous notice, he came out to receive him in a hostile attitude. At a distance of half a league from the city we met two knights, whom Almagro had sent to report his return from Chile, with the intention of bringing help to the besieged. The camps of the two leaders were then pitched at a distance of half a league from each other, and Hernando Pizarro replied that Don Diego de Almagro would be very well received. The governor next morning, without sending an answer to this, marched over some hills near the city, in warlike array, with drums beating and colours flying, to Las Salinas, which is a league from Cuzco. He then sent Juan de Guzman, the Bachiller Guerrero, his secretary Sosa, and two other clerks, named Gonzalo Hernandez and Silva, to require that Hernando Pizarro should comply with the royal provision of your Majesty, for that Cuzco was within the jurisdiction of Almagro.

" Hernando Pizarro complied with the demand, and resigned the government to the municipality of the city, who assembled, together with Captain Hernando Ponçe, the Treasurer Riquelme, the Licentiate Prado, and myself. We all saw the royal provision, and decided that the boundary of the governments was not clearly specified, nor could we decide where it should be. The forces of Almagro then approached nearer, in warlike array, and Hernando Pizarro also began to strengthen his position within the city.

" A truce was then made for three days, but Don Diego de Almagro sent to say that this was on the condition that Hernando Pizarro should not strengthen his position; for that the truce was not made to prepare for fighting, but to confer on terms of peace.

" The following day Don Diego de Almagro entered the town, on the pretext that Hernando Pizarro had broken down some bridges, and was fortifying his camp.[1]  He came in with his whole force and seized Hernando Pizarro, one man being killed on one side, and one on the other.  On coming out of my lodging I met the said Governor Don Diego de Almagro; and, when he was told who I was, he got off his horse, embraced me, and requested me to return to my lodging.  He then took possession of the city; and, having assembled the municipality, he laid before them a report of the pilots, showing that the said city of Cuzco was within the limits of his province, which extended as far as the City of the Kings, where that of Don Francisco Pizarro commenced.  Having examined the report, the municipality unanimously received Don Diego de Almagro as governor of the city; and soon afterwards, on account of the complaints which were made against Hernando Pizarro, a process was commenced against him and his brother, Gonzalo Pizarro, who were prisoners.

"About two months after this, news arrived that a large body of men was approaching from the City of the Kings; and soon afterwards a Spaniard, named Palomino, came from the banks of the river Apurimac, which are eleven leagues from the city, with the tidings that one of the Governor Francisco Pizarro's captains, named Don Alonzo de Alvarado, was coming with five hundred men to succour Cuzco, which was still supposed to be besieged by the Indians; and that, when he heard that the Governor Don Diego de Almagro was in possession of that city, he had fortified himself on the banks of the river Abancay, at a distance of seven or eight leagues from the Apurimac.

---

[1] If this version of the transaction is true, it would seem that Almagro was justified in considering the truce to be at an end.  Further on Don Alonzo asserts still more positively that Hernando caused the bridges to be broken down, and gives the man's name who was employed to do it.  Compare *Helps*, iv, p. 69.  But, on the other hand, Don Alonzo himself is distinctly accused of having betrayed the city to Almagro, in a Royal Order dated March 14th, 1538.  *Varones Illustres*, p. 223.

" The governor sent a deputation to confer with Don Alonzo de Alvarado and his people, consisting of Juan de Guzman, Diego de Mercado, Diego de Alvarado, Gomez de Alvarado, the Licentiate Prado, and myself. We were to inform them, on the part of Don Diego de Almagro, that he was governor of the city of Cuzco by right of the royal decree, which was sent with us, in charge of the clerk of the municipality. We were to add that if they would come under his government, they should receive their share of the land, as vassals of your Majesty; but that if they refused to do so, they must return to the territory of their own governor. Having delivered our message, the said Don Alonzo de Alvarado seized us, and put us all into prison, together with the clerk of the municipality who had come with the royal decree. We were all six loaded with chains, and crowded into a small prison built of stones and mud, where we were kept for thirty days.

" When Don Diego de Almagro heard of the imprisonment of his messengers, he sent an alcalde to demand their liberation; and soon afterwards followed with all the troops he could collect. Don Alonzo de Alvarado still refused to give us up, so the governor attacked him, crossed the river, and took the said Alvarado prisoner. Only five or six men were killed on both sides, and we were released, and returned to Cuzco. Alvarado's men said that he had not shown them the royal decree; and when they saw it they obeyed Don Diego de Almagro, and received him as their governor.

" A month afterwards an embassy arrived from Don Francisco Pizarro, to confer respecting terms of peace, and the release of his brothers. It consisted of the Licentiate Espinosa,[1] Illan Suarez de Carbajal, and Diego de Fuen-

---

[1] The licentiate Gaspar de Espinosa took an important part in the discovery of Peru, having advanced money to Pizarro for his expedition. He fell ill and died at Cuzco, while engaged in these negotiations with Almagro.

mayor, brother of the President of the Audience of San
Domingo.  The Governor Don Diego de Almagro told
them that he desired to send your Majesty's fifth of all the
gold that had been found in the city, together with Hernando
Pizarro, and the accusation against him, to the nearest port,
for transmission to your Majesty.  He then sent Diego
Nuñez de Mercado, the Accountant Juan de Guzman, and
myself, to arrange the boundary between the two provinces,
intending us to embark at the port of Chincha, and proceed
to the City of the Kings with the gold, and the prisoner
Hernando Pizarro.  Accordingly, we arrived in the city of
the Kings, and found the Governor Don Francisco Pizarro
well disposed to peace.  But while we were engaged in
this negociation, Gonzalo Pizarro, the brother of the governor,
and Alonzo de Alvarado escaped from prison, and, with
fifty or sixty horsemen, arrived at the place where we were
conferring respecting the terms of a treaty.  These men
were tired of their imprisonment; they brought promises
and complaints from Hernando Pizarro; they created discord;
they caused the failure of the negociations : and thus they
originated the loss of many lives and much property.  Still,
however, Don Francisco Pizarro continued to treat for some
time longer.

" Don Diego de Almagro named Diego Nuñez de Mercado
and me, as his agents ; and the vice-provincial of the Dominicans, Don Juan de Olias, and Captain Francisco de
Chaves[1] were nominated on the part of Don Francisco
Pizarro.  We met at a place called Mala, which is halfway
between the City of the Kings, where Don Francisco Pizarro
resided, and Chincha, where Don Diego de Almagro was
encamped.[2]  The distance between the City of the Kings

---

[1] There were two knights of this name in Peru, who were cousins.
One of them was murdered in trying to defend Francisco Pizarro from
the assassins.

[2] Almagro marched from Cuzco, through the province of Lucanas, to
the rich coast valley of Nasca, the fertility of which is still entirely due

and Chincha is thirty leagues, along the sea coast. While
we were waiting for fuller powers from the said Don Diego
de Almagro, in order to complete the negociation, a friar interfered, named Francisco de Bobadilla, who was provincial
of the order of our Lady of Mercy. He ruined the whole
plan, and was the principal cause of all the disasters which
followed. The devil must have used the holy dress of this
reverend man as a mask, whereby he might practise his
deceits and lies. He represented that we should never
come to any agreement, but that he would settle the whole
question, and remedy our partiality and long delays. Don
Diego de Almagro only desired to end his life with honour,
and he rejoiced at the offer of the holy friar, deceived by his
sacred calling. He said to him : ' Father, although your
paternity has resided with the governor Don Francisco
Pizarro, yet I believe you to be a faithful servant of our
Lord God, and of his Majesty the Emperor, and I am therefore willing to confide in you, and to place all in your
hands, that you may be the judge of our differences.' The
friar answered that he swore by his habit of our Lady of
Mercy that he would place the boundary at a point which is
twenty leagues nearer Chincha than the City of the Kings.

" Trusting in this promise, Don Diego de Almagro wrote
us a letter, informing us of the confidence he had in the
friar, and saying that, if Don Francisco Pizarro agreed, he
was willing to place every thing in his hands. But the first
thing the friar did was to deprive Don Diego de Almagro of
the city of Cuzco, and to order that Hernando Pizarro
should be released. As soon as he found that he had been
deceived by the friar, Don Diego de Almagro appealed
against his decision ; and the Captains Hernando de Ponce

to works of irrigation of the time of the Incas. He then advanced up
the coast to the valley of Chincha, where he founded a town. Tradition
points out the rich sugar estate of Laran in this valley, now owned by
the hospitable Don Antonio Prada, as the site of Almagro's encampment.

and Francisco de Godoy,[1] honourable men, and friends of
both parties, proposed that the governor Don Diego de
Almagro should evacuate the town of Chincha, and retire
eight leagues further south to a port called San Gallan, to
which port a ship should be sent, in order that he might
dispatch his son with letters informing your Majesty of the
discovery of Chile.

" Don Diego de Almagro accordingly retired to San
Gallan, and formed a town there, appointing alcaldes and
regidores, and erecting a gibbet in the name of your Majesty.[2] He named the place Almagro, and remained there
until he heard that Francisco Pizarro was approaching with
a large force. We then retreated to the *sierra*, and encamped in a strong place called Huaytara;[3] while Don
Francisco Pizarro destroyed the new town, imprisoned the
alcaldes and regidores, and then pursued us. But when we
saw that we could not defend our position without much
risk, we retired to Cuzco, and Don Francisco Pizarro returned to his own City of the Kings.

" Hernando Pizarro marched against us with a large force,
consisting of cavalry, arquebusiers, crossbow men, and six
large pieces of artillery. Don Diego de Almagro had arrived in Cuzco a month before, and, as the roofs of the
houses were made of straw, and the arquebusiers might do
much mischief by setting them on fire, he marched out for
three quarters of a league, with five hundred men, three
hundred cavalry, and two hundred infantry, besides five or

[1] This knight afterwards distinguished himself in the battle of Chupas,
on the side of Vaca de Castro, fighting against the younger Almagro.

[2] This port of San Gallan was no doubt close to the modern Pisco.
There is still an island off the coast called San Gallan. Herrera and
others misspell it *Zangala.*

[3] He marched from the sea port of San Gallan or Pisco, up the valley,
until it became a narrow gorge of the Andes, and encamped in a wild
and inaccessible pass called Huaytara. There is another Huaytara near
Guamanga.

six pieces of artillery.  I remained in the city, because I have always endeavoured not to give offence to any one, neither by word nor deed.  A battle was fought, and Hernando Pizarro gained it, twenty-five or twenty-six men being killed on his side, and one hundred men on that of Don Diego de Almagro, besides fifty badly wounded, and fifty with their faces gashed by their conquerors.  The forces of Hernando Pizarro followed up their victory to the city of Cuzco.

" On the side of Don Diego de Almagro were killed Rodrigo Orgoñez his captain-general, a very valiant knight and faithful servant of your Majesty, and many others.  Don Diego de Almagro, being very infirm, had remained a little in the rear, and when all was over, he fled to the fortress above Cuzco, where he was captured.  Many robberies were committed, although those which came to the notice of Hernando Pizarro were punished; but I can assure your Majesty that on that very night I was taken into the fields by four soldiers, who tormented me for money, and extorted fifty pieces of gold from me, which, however, Hernando Pizarro caused to be restored to me when he heard of it.

" A process was commenced against Don Diego de Almagro which continued for three months.  Finally, Hernando Pizarro sentenced him to death; and, when the sentence was read to him, he was not a little astonished and terrified, exclaiming : ' I appeal to the Emperor and King Don Carlos my lord, whom I have served well and faithfully;' and when this was refused, he said : ' I appeal to the governor your brother.'  When this also was refused, he said : ' Listen to me, Hernando Pizarro.  Remember that I was the first step by which you and your brother rose to power; and that it is not just that you, being my enemy, should put me to death, even if I deserved it.'  He then went down on his knees before him, and, taking a handkerchief from off his head, he said : ' Behold this head, wounded in the ser-

vice of the Emperor our lord! Behold the place where my
eye has been torn out of my face in his service!' Then
Hernando Pizarro replied that he could not do otherwise,
because it was an act of justice, and his followers advised it;
and that such degradation and fear were unworthy of a man
of honour.

"Don Diego de Almagro then said: ' O! sir, remember
that God feared death, and I not only fear death for myself
but on account of my followers.' When he saw that Hernando Pizarro was not moved, and that he was about to
leave him, he exclaimed: ' I appeal to Almighty God, who
is a just judge, and I summon you and all who are accom-
plices in my death, to appear before Him within forty days.'
A friar, who had come to confess him, reproved him for
this speech, saying that it was unlawful for a Christian man
to utter. Don Diego replied that if it was so, he would re-
tract it; and he then confessed like a good Catholic, and
made his will, displaying in his death a strong desire for
life.

" He left your Majesty his heir to all his goods; and
appointed me, as his friend and a servant of your Majesty,
to be his executor, commissioning me to inform your Majesty of the truth. Having confessed and made his will,
they came into his prison to strangle him, when he said:
' I die for having served his Majesty, and I pray to Almighty God that he will pardon you.' They then strangled
him, and carried his body to the plaza, and afterwards it was
buried in the monastery of our Lady of Mercy, Hernando
Pizarro accompanying it with tears and lamentations; which
I believe were not feigned, and that he did this in the
belief that it would be for the good of your service. As to
the question of whether it was just or not, I leave it to the
lawyers.

" Now that I, as executor of Don Diego de Almagro,
have freed him from all blame, I also desire to exculpate

Hernando Pizarro, and not his brother Don Francisco Pizarro, because he is now in the presence of God. As regards Hernando Pizarro, he defended the city of Cuzco when it was besieged by Indians, and acted as a man who really loves your royal person.

" As for myself, considering that your Majesty is obliged to punish the evil, and to reward the good, I request, and, if it be necessary, I demand before God, that you will treat me according to my services ; and I do not seek for mercy, but for justice.

" I must add that it is my belief that if the friar Vicente de Valverde, bishop in Peru, had come to the city of Cuzco, instead of remaining in the City of the Kings, many of the disasters which followed would have been avoided; but I can assure your Majesty that these friars, or at least most of them, as soon as they leave their monasteries, lose all chance of going to heaven.

" I have spoken the truth to your Majesty in this letter, and if I have omitted anything, it has either been to avoid tediousness or scandal; and, if it be necessary, I swear to God, by the habit of Santiago, that everything happened as I have stated. May the same God preserve the royal person of your Majesty, to serve Him, and administer justice.

" I have not given an account of the meeting arranged by the friar provincial in Mala, between the two governors, each accompanied by twelve knights, because it would not be possible to do so with brevity ; and for the same reason I have passed over other events.

" In all things I have endeavoured to serve your Majesty to the best of my power, as I shall continue to do while God gives me life. Most puissant and Christian lord! having served your Majesty for three years, in the conquest of Peru, and in the siege of the great city of Cuzco with the office of master of the camp and captain, at the cost of my estate, and the risk of my life, an order arrived from your Majesty to bring me a prisoner to Spain, and thus I lost the reward of my services in the division (*repartimiento*) of the land. Now I beseech you to reward me in proportion to my services, and I shall always be your loyal servant,

"DON ALONZO ENRIQUEZ DE GUZMAN."

---

## LVII.

THIS IS A LETTER WHICH I WROTE FROM PERU, TO THE MOST ILLUS-
TRIOUS DUKE OF MEDINA SIDONIA, TO WHOM THIS BOOK
IS DEDICATED.

"I beseech you to kiss the hands of the most illustrious lady the Duchess, and to beseech her to remember me, and the dangers of my journeys, in her prayers, for I hold her to be holy and Catholic. I am not able to deny to you that I am not your relation on the Enriquez side, which is the relationship which I value most; but I am of your family through my grandmother, and also through Adam and Eve, our common parents. I likewise desire to kiss the hand of Don Juan Claros, Count of Niebla,[1] to whom I desire you to show this letter, in order to undeceive him; for I have often sworn to him that we are relations on the Enriquez side, but I will do so no more, as it is not true.

"I know well that my brother Don Garcia is more agreeable to you than I am, because he is more prudent; but I am the same relation to you as he is: Don Juan Enriquez, my grandfather, came from Portugal,[2] and married a sister of the Duke your grandfather. Her name was Dona Maria de Guzman, and she was my grandmother. Thus the Duke

---

[1] The duke's eldest son.

[2] Our author's ancestor, the Count of Gijon, settled in Portugal in consequence of his marriage with the Princess Isabella, daughter of Ferdinand, King of that country.

your father, and Don Garcia Enriquez de Guzman my father,
were first cousins; and you and Don Garcia my brother are
second cousins. I declare this to be true, and I have often
been told so by the Duke of Bejar, who is now in glory,
and by the Marshal Gonzalo de Saavedra, as well as by my
father-in-law, and the Añascos his brothers,[1] who are of as
ancient a family as you are. These knights took me for
their relation, when I had not a crust of bread to eat. I do
not wish to give you any farther proof of this, especially as
you do not desire it; but I am consoled to think that when
one door is closed another is opened.

"There is some truth in what you say that I am not your
relation, for the relationship that exists between us is distant,
and in truth scarcely anything, as you say, although my
father was your friend and servant. I was told that we were
relations, and therefore I used your name as my relation, in
all faith and honour. Dated at Cuzco. The last day of
March, 1539."[2]

## LVIII.

A LETTER FROM AN AGED KNIGHT, IN REPLY TO ONE WHICH I HAD
WRITTEN TO HIM, ASKING HIM TO INFORM ME RESPECTING MY
LINEAGE.

"I have received a letter from your worship, in which you
ask me to give you information respecting your genealogy,
which I now send you, from what I have read in the
chronicle of Spain. You are the son of Don Garcia Enriquez de Guzman, whose father was Don Juan Enriquez
your grandfather. Thus you take the name of Enriquez
from your father, and that of Guzman from the wife of this

---

[1] Don Alonzo's wife was Dona Costanza de Añasco.

[2] It would seem that our author had been going about, boasting of
his relationship to the great Duke of Medina Sidonia, until, at last, he
had met with a rebuff; and hence this letter.

Don Juan, whose name was Dona Elvira de Guzman, sister to the Duke of Medina Sidonia. This Don Juan was son of Don Diego Enriquez, Count of Gijon, brother of the King Don Juan; and this is the whole truth, and all that I know about it: and I am, at the service of your worship,

" RUY DIAZ DE GUZMAN."[1]

## LIX.

THIS IS THE ACCUSATION I MADE AGAINST DON HERNANDO PIZARRO, BEFORE THE ROYAL COUNCIL.

" Most puissant Lords,

" I, Don Alonzo Enriquez de Guzman, a knight of the order of Santiago, and gentleman in the royal palace, native of the city of Seville, was appointed executor to the will of Don Diego de Almagro; and, by virtue of that office, I accuse Hernando Pizarro of criminal acts, he who is now a prisoner in this court.[2]

" The Adelantado Don Diego de Almagro, governor of the kingdom of New Toledo, in the Indies of the South Sea, in the province of Peru, laboured in the service of his Majesty, having conquered and settled many kingdoms and provinces in the said land, and converted the people to the service of the Lord God, and of our holy Catholic faith. At this time the said Hernando Pizarro, moved by envy, hatred, and an evil disposition, as well as by avarice and self-interest, drove Mango-ynga into rebellion, whom the said Adelantado

[1] See also notes at pages 5 and 55.
[2] In his former letter to the Emperor, Don Alonzo extenuates and smooths over the worst acts of Hernando Pizarro; while in this statement he does all in his power to blacken his character. Yet, on the whole, he does not pervert facts, and his narrative of events agrees very well with those of the chroniclers of the civil wars in Peru. His motive for speaking well of Hernando to the Emperor, in the first letter, is not very clear, but doubtless it was one of self-interest.

had subjugated, reduced to submission, and induced to sub-
mit to the service of God and his Majesty. This Hernando
Pizarro demanded a great quantity of gold from Capa-ynga,[1]
more than he was able to pay; and for this reason, as well
as on account of many outrages which this Hernando Pizarro
had committed, or allowed to be committed, on this Indian
lord or on his people, he rebelled, and thus your Majesty
lost millions of your revenue, while more than six hundred
Spaniards were killed. I and the said Hernando Pizarro
were besieged in the great city of Cuzco.

" Not content with having perpetrated these crimes, so
horrible and so grave, against your Majesty and the
universal welfare of these kingdoms, he proceeded to
enact further mischief. The Adelantado Don Diego de
Almagro, with five hundred Spaniards, who had gone to
discover other lands, advanced to raise the siege, after
we had been shut up for a whole year. He sent to Hernando Pizarro to inform him that he had come to succour and relieve him, and to execute the orders contained
in the Royal Provision; to which the said Hernando Pizarro
replied, that if he wished to enter the city as the companion
of his brother Francisco, he would be well received, but
that if he intended to take possession of these provinces, he
would be resisted. The Adelantado answered that he was
resolved to execute the royal orders, and it was arranged
that there should be a truce for three days; but the said
Hernando Pizarro secretly ordered the bridges of a river
which flowed through the city to be broken down, and a
man named Cisneros, with two Indians, broke one of the
bridges.[2] On that night I was with Hernando Pizarro, and

---

[1] Inca Manco, son of the great Inca Huayna Ccapac.

[2] See *Herrera*, dec. iv, lib. iv, cap. 1; where it is also asserted that
one of the bridges was broken down, which was clearly a breach of faith
on the part of Hernando Pizarro. On the other hand Don Alonzo was
undoubtedly a traitor to Hernando Pizarro; it is probable that he be-

he said, ' Don Alonzo, let us defend the city as well as we can ;' but, either through spies or by some other means, the Adelantado discovered his intentions, and entered the city. Hernando Pizarro made some resistance with about fifty townsmen and servants of his own, but was taken prisoner.

" Not content with this, the said Hernando Pizarro raised an army and again marched against the said Adelantado, giving him battle near the walls of the city of Cuzco, and killing two hundred and twenty-three men after they had surrendered and were disarmed, some of them in their beds, when re-covering from their wounds.[1] He also illtreated many others by stabbing them in the face, and he cried out in battle, ' Pizarro ! Pizarro !' forgetting God and your Majesty.

" After his victory he entered the city with his troops, and robbed the royal treasury, which was then in charge of Manuel Espina. Then, forgetting the gratitude he owed to the Adelantado, who had released him when he was his prisoner, the said Hernando Pizarro ignominiously strangled the Adelantado Don Diego de Almagro, saying that he was no Adelantado but a vile Moor ; and, in order to increase the insult, he caused a negro to be his executioner ; saying, ' Let not this Moor think that I will give him the death that he would have given me, which was to behead me ;

trayed the city to Almagro, and his version of the affair must therefore be received with some caution.

[1] Hernando Pizarro was not a party to any of these atrocities. Many excesses were, however, committed by his soldiers ; and the murder of Pedro de Lerma, who had fought hand to hand with Hernando, in the battle of Las Salinas, was especially atrocious. He was lying ill of his wounds, in a house at Cuzco, when a cowardly villain named Samaniego came into his room, and said, " I come, in satisfaction of my honour, to kill you for a box on the ear which you once gave me." He then basely murdered him with a dagger; for which deed he was himself hanged, by the Governor of Puerto Viejo, five years afterwards. *G. de la Vega*, pte. ii, lib. ii, cap. 38.

and I declare that if the knife was raised to cut off my head, and the gates of hell open, and the devil ready to receive me, I would still do what I am now doing.' To add to the indignity, after the rope was round the neck of the Adelantado, it was allowed to remain on the body for two hours. I also was taken into the fields in the middle of the night by five arquebusiers, who tormented me with a cord round my wrists until the blood came out under my nails ; and I was robbed of six thousand *castellanos* in gold and silver and clothes. The torments and robbery were inflicted upon me by order of the said Hernando Pizarro.[1] This took place on the night of the eve of St. Lazarus, in the year 1538, being the same day on which Hernando Pizarro defeated the Adelantado Don Diego de Almagro. Not content with having thus outraged and insulted a gentleman of noble lineage, this Hernando Pizarro ordered a soldier of his party to kill me whenever he found an opportunity. This man, whose name was Bosque, with four others, climbed into the house of Felipe Gutierrez, where I was, and gave me so many sword cuts that they left me for dead. Hernando Pizarro dissembled, and showed no zeal whatever in capturing these men, just as a man would act if he had ordered them to do it.[2]

"In the battle this Hernando Pizarro and his people killed Juan Fernandez de Silva, who owed me 2,500 *castellanos* for a horse, which they stole, besides having robbed me of 14,000 *castellanos* which I had placed for safety in the house of the Adelantado.

"Hernando Pizarro killed the Adelantado against all justice, and without any authority; I received injury from him to

[1] In his letter to the Emperor he acknowledges that Hernando Pizarro caused his money to be restored to him, when he heard of the robbery. See *ante*, p. 150.

[2] Here, too, a different version of the story is given. Compare the account of the same affair given at p. 130.

the amount of 2,000 *castellanos*; and for his atrocious and wicked crimes and treasons it is right that he should receive punishment."[1]

---

## LX.

### HOW THE EMPEROR WOULD NEITHER SEE NOR LISTEN TO ME, WHEN HE CAME FROM ITALY IN THE YEAR 1542.

The Emperor came to visit his children and to hold his court in these kingdoms, but his return was so rapid that he had embarked again at Barcelona for Italy before I could reach the port.[2] The most serene and most excellent Prince Philip, our natural lord, was in Madrid; and he told Don Fernando Alvarez de Toledo, Duke of Alva, and mayo-domo of his royal house, to direct me to write to the Emperor. This nobleman was my very good friend, as was also his grandfather of glorious memory, Don Fadrique de Toledo, whom I have already mentioned in this book.[3] Seeing that I was miserable, the most serene Prince consoled me, saying —" Do not be troubled, Don Alonzo, for the Emperor my father wishes you no evil; and he was unable to see you, because he had many things to arrange before his embarka-

[1] Another and probably more influential attack was made on Hernando Pizarro, when he arrived in Spain, by Don Diego de Alvarado, the old friend of Almagro. Hernando Pizarro sailed from Lima in the summer of 1539, and, passing through Mexico, reached Valladolid in 1540. He was coldly received at court, and shortly afterwards, owing probably to the accusations of Diego de Alvarado, our author, and other friends of Almagro, was imprisoned in the castle of Medina del Campo, where he remained in confinement for twenty-three years. He was at length discharged in 1563, an aged and disappointed man, having outlived both friends and enemies. He retired to his native town, where he died, after attaining to the extreme age of one hundred years.

[2] He left his son Philip as Regent, assisted by Tabara, Archbishop of Toledo, the Secretary Francisco de los Cobos, and the Duke of Alva.

[3] See pages 54, 60, and 74.

tion." This consoled me greatly; and afterwards the Grand
Commander of Leon wrote to my lady his wife to tell her
that the Emperor had said that I was with his son, which
showed that he was not displeased with me.

## LXI.

### OF THE PRINCE DON PHILIP.

· Don Philip, the prince of Spain, attained the age of sixteen in the year 1542.[1]   He is very handsome, with very
white face and hands, and with the best disposition of any
creature whom God has made.   Very sagacious, intelligent,
pious, and orderly, taking care that everything shall be done
in its proper place and time.   Above all, he is a good Christian, which is the principal thing.   This prince, finding that
I had suffered imprisonments and persecutions from the
Emperor his father, took me into favour while the Emperor
was absent from Spain, for he had been informed by the good
knights of his household, how I had served his father against
Moors and Frenchmen, with the rank of captain.   These
knights were the illustrious Don Juan de Zuñiga,[2] second son
of the Count of Miranda, Don Antonio de Rojas, Don Alvaro
de Cordova, Don Manrique de Silva, and Ruy Gomez, a Portuguese knight of noble family.   They all assisted me to the
favour of the prince; so that, from the time that he attained
the age of sixteen, he always loved and favoured me, and I
owe this chiefly to Don Juan de Zuñiga, who was Grand
Commander of Castile.   He was one of the most honourable

[1] He was born at Valladolid on May 21st, 1527.   At the age of seven
Charles V gave him a separate establishment.

[2] He taught his pupil to fence, ride, and tilt, and encouraged him to
invigorate his frame by the hardy pleasures of the chase.   *Prescott's
Philip II*, i, p. 27.

knights in the kingdom, and was so well fitted for this office that, without being tedious or troublesome, he kept the Prince well instructed, though the Prince himself assisted with his clear head. The Commander, hat in hand, told the Prince that he was not to do more than he wished; while his Highness gave the Commander to understand that he would do all that he desired.

## LXII.

### HOW THE PRINCE GOES FROM MADRID TO ALCALA, TO SEE THE INFANTAS HIS SISTERS, AND HOW HE TOOK ME WITH HIM.

His Highness learnt that I was going to Saragossa, to the wedding of Don Diego de los Cobos, son of the grand Commander of Leon, Don Francisco de los Cobos, and of his excellent wife, my lady; and he said to me : " Don Alonzo, before you set out with Dona Maria de Mendoza, you must come with me for eight days to visit my sisters."[1] I therefore went with him, and, during all these eight days, I was with him and the ladies his sisters, playing with them and diverting them, no one else being present. I found in the Lady Infanta Dona Maria a repetition of her brother, both in person and disposition; and I will say no more, because what I have already said of her brother, equally applies to her. At last, I took leave of this most serene and excellent prince, he going to Valladolid, and I returning to Madrid on my way to Saragossa.

I was very sorry to part with the prince, and he felt the same towards me. Soon afterwards, the wife of Don Fran-

[1] The daughters of the Emperor Charles V were Maria, married to her cousin the Emperor Maximilian II, and Juana, married to her cousin Don Juan the Prince of Portugal. Juana was the mother of Sebastian of Portugal, who was killed in the battle of Alcazar, fighting the Moors, in 1578.

cisco de los Cobos set out for the kingdom of Aragon, to
celebrate the marriage of her son; but, for some evil sound-
ing words which I had used, an inquisitor in Seville ordered
me to be confined in a monastery for thirty days, and he
gave me a penance, which was that I should give ten ducats
to a hospital.

## LXIII.

### WHAT HAPPENED TO ME WITH A LADY OF MADRID, IN THE MONTH OF MAY, 1543.

You must know that there is a lady of noble lineage and
honourable life, in Madrid, named Dona Maria de Ulloa,[1] a
widow, and mother of the Count of Salinas. She has three
granddaughters in her house, very honourable and beautiful,
and of tender age, though not so young as to be unable to
marry. One is a daughter of the Count of Rivagorça, Dona
Mariana de Aragon,[2] a lady who was in the household of the
empress our lady, now in glory. She is so beautiful, so
discreet, and so courageous that, in truth, I have never met
any one, excepting the most illustrious lady Dona Maria de
Mendoza, with whom she can be compared. One night I
went to see her grandmother in Santo Domingo el Real,
where she lives; and this Dona Mariana said to me : " Señor
Don Alonzo, have you seen the altars of the lady Dona
Maria de Ulloa, my grandmother, in this house?" I replied : " No, lady." She then said : " Do you wish me to
show them to you?" I answered : " When your ladyship

[1] This lady was a daughter of Don Rodrigo de Ulloa, Alcaide of Toro
and Lord of Mota, a renowned knight in the wars of Granada, by Aldonza
de Castilla, great granddaughter of Peter the Cruel. She married Don
Diego Perez Sarmiento de Villandrando, Count of Salinas.

[2] Dona Maria de Ulloa's daughter Ana married Don Alonzo de Aragon,
Count of Ribagorça.

pleases," thinking it would be on some other day.   But she
rose up quickly, and told a page to take a candle and walk
on in front, while she and I followed, and no one besides.
We passed through manў chambers and anterooms, and
along several corridors where there was a very high wind,
and I trembled lest the candle should be blown out.   I
called out to the page to take care of the light; and thus we
came to the altars, which are three in number.   I went to
the centre one, because I thought it would look most
devout, and recited an Ave Maria, that being the shortest
prayer I knew.   I then said to an image of the Mother of
God: " Lady, by the joy which you felt when the angel
told you that the Lord was with you, succour me, and give
me joy and happiness."

Then a dueña came in, and I swear by God that I thought
she had fallen from heaven, and still think so, for I had seen
all the dueñas in the household of Dona Maria de Ulloa, and
this one was never amongst them.   On another day, I went
with my lady Doña Maria to dine at this house, and remained all day with these ladies.   I then said to the young
lady Mariana : " I rejoice that you are come, for indeed we
were very solitary without you."   But, as the devil never
sleeps, and as the lady was determined to enjoy my confusion, she replied : " Don Alonzo, I would have you to know
that nothing ever goes wrong except when a dueña is present; for then a man of flesh and blood suffers such torments
of fear and shame that I quite pity him."   After this I
made haste to go to the room where her grandmother and
cousins were sitting ; and may God guard me from being
left alone with her again.   Amen.   Amen.

## LXIV.

WE ARRIVE AT ALCALA, AND HOW THE ARCHBISHOP OF TOLEDO GAVE
ME A WARNING.

On Thursday the 17th of May, 1543, I set out with the most excellent lady Dona Maria de Mendoza, to be present at the marriage of her son. We arrived at Alcala de Henares, where the daughters of the Emperor resided. We found their highnesses very desirous to see my lady, and she lodged in their company, and in that of their ladies, whose names were Doña Ana de Zuñiga, Doña Beatriz de Melo, Doña Leonora Marcarena, Doña Isabel Osorio, Doña Luisa de Viamonte, Doña Catalina de Robles, Doña Maria de Castro, and Doña Ana de Guzman. We were very well received, and the doors of their highnesses were always open to us, although they were closed to every other human creature, excepting at dinner and supper time. I entered at other times, with my lady, and played at ball and at other games with their highnesses, with much pleasant conversation.

You must know that this intimacy which I enjoy with the Prince and his sisters arises from the love which I feel for them, and not from any motives of interest or of avarice. Seeing this intimacy, Don Juan Tabara, the Cardinal Archbishop of Toledo (whom I love as much for his infinite goodness, as because I was brought up with him under the Archbishop of Seville of glorious memory), took me aside and said, " Don Alonzo, I would have you to remember that we live in an envious world, do not therefore give the envious any occasion to speak ill of you ;" besides many other things which, to avoid being tedious, I omit. I replied, " I kiss the hands of your most reverend paternity, but in truth I do not deem it necessary to take so much care about such a trifle."[1]

---

[1] Tabara, the Cardinal Archbishop of Toledo, died in 1544. " He was an excellent man, and greatly valued by the Emperor, who may be

## LXV.

We started from Madrid, and were twenty days on the road, and met with a grand reception on entering the city of Saragossa. The Grand Commander of Leon, the Duke of Alva, the Viceroy, the Count of Aranda, the Count of Nieva, and the Archbishop, with many other persons, came out for five leagues to meet us, not counting those who came as spectators. In the entrances to the *plaza* there were three triumphal arches; and, in the evening, a great company of knights and beautiful ladies were entertained at supper. These feasts, dances, jousts, tilting matches, and bull fights, continued for six days.

Afterwards I went to Valladolid with the Grand Commander of Leon and the Duke of Alva, and was very well received by the best Prince that God ever gave to us. Here I was challenged to a match in the tilt yard, by Don Juan de Mendoza, a brother of my lady, ten of a side. On his side was the Duke of Alva, and I requested the Prince to be on mine. He replied that he was not dexterous in the exercises of the tilt yard; but he consented at last, and played so well that, if he had been the son of a shoemaker, he would have deserved the prize. I was dressed in his colours, which are brown and white; while the opposite side wore blue and red; and I wrote the following challenge :—

thought to have passed a sufficient encomium on his worth when he declared that ' by his death Philip had suffered a greater loss than by that of Mary of Portugal, for he could get another wife, but not another Tabara.' "—*Prescott's Philip II*, vol. i, p. 38.

[1] He married Dona Francisca Luisa de Luna, heiress of Camarasa. Their child succeeded his grandmother Dona Maria, as Count of Riba-dabia.

"I, Don Alonzo Enriquez de Guzman, declare that a cartel was presented to me by Don Juan de Mendoza, proposing that he, with nine knights, should tilt against me and nine other knights. I accept the challenge in order that each knight may be able to display the valour of his person, so that, when the ladies come, he may be esteemed and honoured by them." Certain rules were then published, and umpires were appointed; and, as I have told you before, the Prince distinguished himself above all the other knights.

The sides were as follows—

| | |
|---|---|
| The Prince our Lord | The Duke of Alva |
| Don Hernando de Castro | Don Luis Manrique |
| The Prince of Asculi | The Count of Altamera |
| Don Antonio de Toledo | Don Inigo de Guevara |
| Don Antonio de Rojas | The Marquis of Camarasa |
| Don Diego de Azevedo | Don Juan de Benavides |
| Ruy Gomez | Don Juan de Mendoza |
| Don Alonzo Enriquez de Guzman | |

Each knight was to give his opponent four blows with the pike, and four with the sword; and afterwards they were to observe the same order in the mêlée, according to the following rules—

The knight who shall fall from a blow with a sword wins nothing.

He who falls from a blow with a pike wins nothing.

In the mêlée the same rules shall be observed.

The knight who fights best with the sword shall win a sword.

The knight who fights best with the pike shall win a dozen pairs of gloves.

He who fights best with the sword in the mêlée shall win a leathern shield.

He who fights best with the pike in the mêlée shall win the prize.

I appointed as umpires the Grand Commanders of Leon and of Castile, and Don Sancho de Cordova, to judge and decide who were the winners.

---

## LXVI.

THIS IS A LETTER WHICH A KNIGHT OF SEVILLE, NAMED PERO MEXIA, WROTE TO THE AUTHOR OF THIS BOOK, IN REPLY TO OTHERS WHICH HE HAD SENT TO HIM.

" You do me so much honour in writing to me, that I feel that I do not deserve so much attention, but be satisfied that I feel and know the favour that you do me. I saw the letters of Don Pedro de Cordova, and that which you wrote to the lady Infanta. Your letter appeared to me to be very discreet and acute ; and I gather from the other letters that you are appreciated as you deserve. Some say that the prince began to delight in your company on account of your witty conversation ; others declare that you are an honourable knight of ability and good lineage, and that princes favour such men without the aid of wit. Those who write to you otherwise from Seville do ill, for if they are friends they should not say such things, even if they are true. I have written to you twice, but I fear my letters have been lost, as you make no mention of them ; yet I can scarcely believe this, as I gave them to the Accountant Zarate."[1]

[1] Augustin de Zarate was Comptroller of Accounts for Castile from 1528 to 1543. In 1544 he went to Peru in the train of the Viceroy Blasco Nuñez de Vela, to hold the same office in that rich colony. On his return Charles V gave him a similar appointment in Flanders. He wrote a history of the conquest of Peru, and subsequent civil wars down

168 THE LIFE AND ACTS, ETC.

[NOTE.

*Then follow several pages which are quite illegible, owing to the paper having been blotted over with ink ; but this letter appears to be the end of the manuscript, which thus concludes quite abruptly.*]

to the time of Gasca, which first appeared at Antwerp in 1555. Zarate's work is one of the most valuable authorities on this portion of history, and is largely quoted by Garcilasso de la Vega.

FINIS.

For EU product safety concerns, contact us at Calle de José Abascal, 56–1°, 28003 Madrid, Spain or eugpsr@cambridge.org.